In the Shadow of a Rugged Cross

In the Shadow of a Rugged Cross

Reflections on the Spirituality of Dietrich Bonhoeffer

CHARLES R. RINGMA

CASCADE Books • Eugene, Oregon

IN THE SHADOW OF A RUGGED CROSS
Reflections on the Spirituality of Dietrich Bonhoeffer

Copyright © 2025 Charles R. Ringma. All rights reserved. Except for brief quotations in critical publications or reviews, no part of this book may be reproduced in any manner without prior written permission from the publisher. Write: Permissions, Wipf and Stock Publishers, 199 W. 8th Ave., Suite 3, Eugene, OR 97401.

Cascade Books
An Imprint of Wipf and Stock Publishers
199 W. 8th Ave., Suite 3
Eugene, OR 97401

www.wipfandstock.com

PAPERBACK ISBN: 979-8-3852-1811-0
HARDCOVER ISBN: 979-8-3852-1812-7
EBOOK ISBN: 979-8-3852-1813-4

Cataloguing-in-Publication data:

Names: Ringma, Charles R., author.

Title: In the shadow of a rugged cross : reflections on the spirituality of Dietrich Bonhoeffer / Charles R. Ringma.

Description: Eugene, OR: Cascade Books, 2025 | Includes bibliographical references.

Identifiers: ISBN 979-8-3852-1811-0 (paperback) | ISBN 979-8-3852-1812-7 (hardcover) | ISBN 979-8-3852-1813-4 (ebook)

Subjects: LCSH: Bonhoeffer, Dietrich, 1906–1945—Meditations.

Classification: BX4827 R47 2025 (paperback) | BX4827 (ebook)

04/25/25

All Scripture quotations, unless otherwise indicated, are taken from the New Revised Standard Version Bible, copyright 1989, Division of Christian Education of the National Council of the Churches of Christ in the United States of America. Used by permission. All rights reserved.

For

Faculty, staff, and students at
Asian Theological Seminary (Metro Manila)
and
all seminaries in the Majority World that seek to integrate
theological (head), spiritual (heart), and missional formation (hands).

Contents

Preface		xi
Introduction		xv
1	A Spirituality of Vulnerability	1
	1:1 Living Through Anxious Times	3
	1:2 Identifying with Others	6
	1:3 Expectant Listening	8
	1:4 Praying Through Difficulties	11
	1:5 Following the "Hidden" Christ	13
	1:6 Facing Disappointment	16
2	A Spirituality of Joining	19
	2:1 Living In Christ	21
	2:2 Joining the Suffering Christ	23
	2:3 Joining the Suffering Church	26
	2:4 Joining the Suffering of the World	29
	2:5 Joining the Poor	31
	2:6 Joining God's Kingdom Purposes	34
3	Sustained by the Faith Community	37
	3:1 The Living Word	40
	3:2 The Sacramental Life: Baptism	42
	3:3 The Sacramental Life: Holy Communion	44
	3:4 Worship: A Way of Life	47
	3:5 Life Together	50
	3:6 Witness and Service	52

Contents

4 Sustained by the Spirit — 55
- 4:1 Bound to Christ — 58
- 4:2 Comfort in Times of Difficulty — 61
- 4:3 Discernment — 63
- 4:4 Empowerment — 65
- 4:5 In-Spirited — 68
- 4:6 True Spirit for This Age — 71

5 Sustained by Spiritual Practices — 74
- 5:1 Prayer — 76
- 5:2 Scripture — 79
- 5:3 Faith — 82
- 5:4 Friendship — 85
- 5:5 Vulnerability and Confession — 88
- 5:6 Suffering — 90

6 Resisting the Powers — 93
- 6:1 Keeping Step with a Different Drummer — 96
- 6:2 Discerning When to Say, "No" — 98
- 6:3 Living the Christ Reality — 101
- 6:4 Faith Steeled by Courage — 103
- 6:5 Sharing in Christ's Suffering — 106
- 6:6 A Prophetic Way of Life — 108

7 A Prophetic Spirituality — 111
- 7:1 The Call of God — 114
- 7:2 The Shaping of Life — 116
- 7:3 Into the Struggle — 119
- 7:4 Confronting the Powers — 122
- 7:5 A New Vision — 124
- 7:6 Vicarious Suffering — 126

8 Engaging Society — 129
- 8:1 God's Heart for the World — 131
- 8:2 The Gift of Discernment — 134
- 8:3 Radical Identification — 137
- 8:4 Prophetic Witness — 139

Contents

	8:5	Discipleship Service	141
	8:6	Power of Hope	143
9	Celebrating the Good in Our World		146
	9:1	The Gift of Family	149
	9:2	The Gift of Learning	151
	9:3	The Gift of Creativity	154
	9:4	A New Humanity: Bound by Love	157
	9:5	A Global and Ecumenical Church	159
	9:6	Future Hope	161
10	A Spirituality of Hope		164
	10:1	The Gift of Hope	166
	10:2	The Power of Hope	168
	10:3	The Struggles of Hope	170
	10:4	Broken Dreams	173
	10:5	Always on the Way	175
	10:6	God's Final Future	177
Afterword			179
Bibliography			181

Preface

As we come to the end of this first quarter of the twenty-first century, we are facing difficult and challenging times. With climate change, we are seeing the disappearance of plant and animal life and troubled by more severe weather events. We are experiencing pandemics and encountering the rise of violent extremism. We are living with employment insecurities as well as greater poverty and injustice in our world. And we are facing the uncertain changes that virtual intelligence will bring, along with significant shifts in global political alignments.

As we live with these and many other distressing realities, we often feel powerless, overwhelmed, and fearful. Such feelings may cause us to question our faith and our ability to trust in God's care and love for us and the world.

While we have to make our own way as we seek to navigate these days of opportunity and threat, we can also draw encouragement from others who have lived through difficult times. One such person is Dietrich Bonhoeffer—a pastor, theologian, and activist—who sought to follow Jesus as he lived through all the challenges of World War II while opposing Hitler's Nazi regime.

This book is series of reflections on the spirituality that sustained Bonhoeffer until his fateful execution just before the end of the war.

There is little doubt that the writings, life, and example of Dietrich Bonhoeffer will continue to make an impact on all who dip into his well-known books, which include *The Cost of Discipleship*, *Life Together*, and *Letters and Papers from Prison*, along with those who read a biography on his life or encounter his theological and ethical discussions.

But as we engage Bonhoeffer, it is important to keep in mind that there are varying interpretations of his life and work. Some see him primarily as a theologian who promoted a theology for the secular world. Others see him as a political activist who resisted Hitler's Nazi regime. Some see him primarily as pastor who served various congregations and trained clergy for the Confessing Church in Germany. And others see him as a saint who reflected deeply on the Sermon on the Mount and who lived a christological spirituality.[1]

Much debate and discussion will undoubtedly continue about Bonhoeffer's life and writings, but I have a different focus in this book. In these pages, I am seeking *inspiration* from Bonhoeffer's life and writings that can encourage us for the challenges we must face in our time. While Bonhoeffer faced a different juggernaut, we can learn from him as he sought to follow the way of Christ amidst the precarious circumstances of his time. Like us, he struggled with anxiety, family matters, the church, and the political situation of his day, and he also faced issues regarding prayer, faithfulness, suffering, witness, and service.

Since my early twenties, I have read and reread the writings of Bonhoeffer. Each time I return to his work, I find new sources of hope and encouragement. And while I have taught and written on Bonhoeffer over the years,[2] this book represents a renewed engagement with his work in the light of the COVID-19 pandemic and other crises we are facing. In the future, who knows what other pandemics and difficulties we may have to face? But once again, we can draw fresh encouragement from Bonhoeffer.

I hope that you will find renewed faith and courage in these pages.

Major sections of this book were written while I was on retreat in a Polish Monastery near Canungra, Queensland, Australia, along with some of my writing companions. We irreverently call ourselves the "holy scribblers," and we are: Irene Alexander, Chris Brown, Terry Gatfield, Athena Gorospe, Stephanie Maher, Jill Manton, Tim McCowan, Ross McKenzie, Paul Mercer, and Sarah Nicholl.[3]

I am once again deeply indebted to Karen Hollenbeck Wuest for her editorial finesse. I sometimes wonder whether Karen understands me

---

1. For some of that discussion, the following may be helpful: Bethge, *Dietrich Bonhoeffer*; de Gruchy, ed., *Cambridge Companion to Dietrich Bonhoeffer*; Haynes, *Bonhoeffer Phenomenon*.

2. My writings on Bonhoeffer include: *Seize the Day with Dietrich Bonhoeffer*; "A Critical Evaluation of the Ecclesiology of Dietrich Bonhoeffer"; "Dietrich Bonhoeffer: His Life, Theology, Praxis with Implications for Ecumenism"; "In the World and Sore Afraid"; and "Bonhoeffer's Passion for Renewing the Church and its Witness in Troubled Times."

3. See our blogspot: https://holyscribblers.blogspot.com.

Preface

better than I know myself. I see her delightful skill in almost every page! And a hearty thanks to my literary agent, Pieter Kwant, who demonstrates an amazing tenacity in getting my books into print.

Charles Ringma
Brisbane, Australia
2024

Introduction

THIS BOOK IS COMPRISED of a series of topical reflections on the spirituality of Dietrich Bonhoeffer. By "spirituality," I do not mean an exclusive focus on the inner life, though a person's prayer life and personal spiritual practices are certainly part of one's spirituality. Because Bonhoeffer was profoundly christological, these reflections have a Christian spirituality in view: the faithful following of Jesus through the enabling Holy Spirit. Christian spirituality encompasses a whole way of life that is lived to the glory of God as part of the life of the church, in family, in daily work, and for the well-being of the neighbor.

We can readily identify several major themes in Bonhoeffer's spirituality.

First, Bonhoeffer was captivated by the person and work of Jesus Christ. He believed that Christ is relevant in shaping the inner disposition of our being and should be the center of our life orientation, affecting every domain of life (including the political) through our witness and service. As the icon of the new humanity, Christ is to be followed in a costly discipleship that will lead to reconciliation, peacemaking, human well-being, and the restoration of all things. For Bonhoeffer, Christ is not merely an add-on to a person's life, nor is he contained in the church. Rather, he is the center of all of life and history.

Second, Bonhoeffer's christological spirituality was characterized by the maintenance of various spiritual practices, including *Lectio Divina*, prayer, meditation, the ecclesiastical disciplines of proclamation and the sacraments, and a daring activism marked by a prophetic intent to expose evil and herald the good news of God's justice. For Bonhoeffer, contemplation and action constitute a single melody line: piety merges with the quest for justice, prayer with service, and faith with suffering.

Third, Bonhoeffer's spirituality, while profoundly personal, was generously communal rather than individualistic. He believed in communal spiritual practices and communal witness, but his concern was for the church as a whole to be an expression of Christ. The church, as a secondary "incarnation" of Christ, should emulate Christ, embody Christ's way in the world, and live as a sign of what a new world could look like. Thus life together, cooperation, and practical ecumenism were important themes for Bonhoeffer.

Fourth, Bonhoeffer saw Jesus as the "man for others" and advocated a prophetic spirituality. While the faith community is to live for the glory of God and the well-being of its members, its calling is to bring the world into the generative and birthing purposes of God. Thus the church should not be an idle bystander in the affairs of society, but an active participant. Its task is to bear costly prophetic witness to the world by challenging the idolatrous pretensions of the state and questioning the dominant values of a society. In the church's life together, witness, and service, it is called to demonstrate that a new way and a new life is possible. Bonhoeffer sought to bring the words and way of Christ out of the sanctuary and into the maelstrom of political life by raising his voice against political idolatry, racism, genocide, and warmongering.

Fifth, Bonhoeffer's spirituality was never utopian. He highly regarded the importance of family and good social institutions, and he longed to see all of society flourish. Thus he sought to promote a world-formative spirituality rather than a world-denying way of being in the world. He did not believe that we could bring heaven to earth, but that we could bring earth to heaven by living the whole of our lives in the light of the glory and grace of God.

Sixth, Bonhoeffer believed that one of the true marks of Christian spirituality is to embrace victims of oppression, the weak, and the marginalized. While he believed that God has a heart for all (including the conversion of the oppressors), followers of Jesus are called to side with the poor and advocate on their behalf. Bonhoeffer saw this downward spirituality in the life and work of Jesus, whom Bonhoeffer sought to emulate.

Finally, Bonhoeffer's writings mention the call to redemptive suffering. Just as Christ suffered for the sins of others, his followers are called to live and pray redemptively on behalf of others. Put simply, this may mean taking upon oneself the shame and folly of others in order to "undo" the wrong they have done through acts of healing and restoration.

Introduction

In the following chapters, I hope we will gain a richer impression of the spirituality that Bonhoeffer lived and encouraged all Christ followers to embrace.[1]

I should note that Bonhoeffer's writings cannot be nicely compartmentalized, for these themes are integrated in all of his work. Thus his Christology is concerned with ecclesiology, and his commitment to prayer is connected with service. For though prayer is a personal spiritual practice, it is also at the heart of the life and mission of the church—which has everything to do with life in and for the world. As a consequence, some repetition will occur.

I trust that the reader will note a sense of urgency in these pages. Like Bonhoeffer, we are living in challenging times. To navigate these times, we need to grow in fidelity to Christ and become more fully formed in him. Our faith communities need to find new ways to worship and cultivate life together. And our witness to the world needs to become more embodied and prophetic.

So let us join with Bonhoeffer in the hope that "God will cause grace and compassion to radiate over the dark guilt of our century and the human race."[2] May we give the Holy Spirit "full space within us" so that we may live "for the sake of God, for the sake of others, and for our sake."[3]

While this book can be used for personal daily reflections or a personal retreat, it can also be used by those who work together in the faith community, in Christian organizations, or in secular occupations. May this serve as a guide for reflective time together as you seek to hear and reflect on the challenges that Bonhoeffer brings. May the Spirit inspire our collective witness and service in our time.

---

1. For a scholarly discussion of Bonhoeffer's spirituality, see Kelly and Nelson, *Cost of Moral Leadership*.
2. Bonhoeffer, *Works*, vol. 10, *Barcelona, Berlin, New York 1928–1931*, 359.
3. Bonhoeffer, *Works*, vol. 16, *Conspiracy and Imprisonment 1940–1945*, 628.

I

A Spirituality of Vulnerability

Introduction

IT MAY SEEM STRANGE to begin a reflective reader on the spirituality of Dietrich Bonhoeffer with the topic of vulnerability, but this is most appropriate for the times in which we are living.

Not all that long ago, we in the Western world lived with a great sense of confidence and security. We thought that life could only get better and more prosperous—ignoring, of course, that many living in the Majority World of Asia, Africa, and South America were living a far more precarious and challenging existence.

But at this point in the twenty-first century, things are looking quite different for all of us. The global financial crisis, the COVID-19 pandemic, the ongoing challenges of climate change, a future with greater reliance on artificial intelligence, the persistence of fascism, and the convulsions of changing "empires" have left many of us feeling much more vulnerable.

When we add the issues of fragile families, employment insecurities, untrustworthy social institutions, and skepticism about politics, it is no wonder that we are in state of existential crisis. We seem to feel internally threatened and uncertain, with little secure ground under our feet. And when we overlay all of this with the "seeming virtuosity" of the relativism of postmodern thinking, there seems to be little light for navigating the way forward.

Of course, when we think about this a little more carefully, we may well have to conclude that life itself is most vulnerable—and to think otherwise is mere folly, delusion, or escapism. For at any moment, anything can happen to us: sickness, loss, discouragement. And anything may suddenly come our way: a typhoon, a troubling change of government, military conflict, an economic crisis, a plague. At a more basic personal level, there awaits for all of us the vulnerabilities of aging, with the eventual plunge into irrelevance and possible neglect. Death may well be a welcome relief in such circumstances.

Even for people of faith, things are not fundamentally different. While faith and trust in God can bring comfort and the hope of fullness of life in God's final future, Christians are not cocooned from any of these distressing realities. The Christian lives "in Christ," but also in the world—with all its beauty, challenges, and difficulties.

Dietrich Bonhoeffer was no exception. Although he was born into a privileged family and lived as a Christian, pastor, and theologian, he experienced the political and economic instability of Germany after World War I, the rise of fascism, the madness of Hitler's Third Reich, and the tragedy of World War II.

To live in more reflective and vulnerable ways amidst the difficulties of our time, as Bonhoeffer did, is not a sign of weakness. But if we attempt to live with a "steely" self-sufficiency, we deny our basic humanity, and life may crush us—for after all, we are creatures.

Thus vulnerability is common ground for all of us. And instead of trying to avoid vulnerability, we may need to face it, embrace it, learn from it, and allow its generative impulses to transform us.

1:1

Living Through Anxious Times

My anguish, my anguish! I writhe in pain!
Oh, the walls of my heart!
My heart is beating wildly;
I cannot keep silent;
for I hear the sound of the trumpet,
the alarm of war.

—JEREMIAH 4:19

The prophet Jeremiah, often called the "weeping prophet," had visions of the terrible things that the people of Israel were going to experience.

Similarly, Dietrich Bonhoeffer was able to anticipate and warn others of the tragic things that lay ahead for Germany under the new leadership of Adolf Hitler. Very early in this tragic drama, he publicly criticized Hitler's distortion of the concept of leadership.

Bonhoeffer went on to speak of the fear "in Germany," in "our own lives," and "in the nave of the church," pointing out that fear "takes away a person's humanity" and can grow to the point where "we don't even want to find a way out."[1] In his later writings, he acknowledges that "difficulties are magnified out of all proportion . . . by fear and anxiety."[2]

He also spoke of the "destructive effects of prolonged personal insecurity" and was deeply concerned that so many people had "so little ground under [their] feet" in responding to life's difficulties.[3]

---

1. From a sermon Bonhoeffer delivered on January 15, 1933, titled, "Overcoming Fear." Quoted in Best, ed., *Collected Sermons*. Accessed online, https://politicaltheology.com/overcoming-fear-sermon-dietrich-bonhoeffer.
2. Bonhoeffer, *Letters and Papers*, 177.
3. Bonhoeffer, *Letters and Papers*, 16, 3.

Though our time and circumstances are different, we can identify with Bonhoeffer's concerns.

Anxiety can embed itself deeply into the core of our being, especially for those who have more vulnerable dispositions. In our time, particularly in the West, anxiety has become an acute problem because we live in a culture of claiming our rights and making demands, and we often have unreal expectations along with a ballooning sense of entitlement. When things don't readily fall into our lap, or when our demands are not fulfilled, we can easily spiral into anxiety as well as anger.

Moreover, with the ongoing impacts of the coronavirus pandemic and other global challenges, our entire world is marked by fear and anxiety, and many are suffering from mental health issues. Together, these struggles constitute an avalanche of suffering and dislocation.

In the Gospels, Jesus exhorts his disciples, "do not be afraid" (Matt 14:27) and, "do not worry about your life" (Matt 6:25). But Christians are often marked by worries and anxieties, for they partake of the realities of the human condition and are not shielded from the mishaps, follies, and tragedies of life.

Moreover, Christians may well experience anxieties that others don't have, since they may be anxious about their faith, lack of prayer, or the seeming weakness of their relationship with God. They may be anxious about family members who are not walking the faith journey, or they may feel worried about their own ineffective witness. They may also be anxious about what is happening in the world, with God being increasingly pushed to the margins and the church no longer holding its place as a significant institution in society. Thus, for many Christians, a deep sense of concern may deteriorate into deep anxiety or despair.

There are no magical answers to these issues—and to "beat ourselves up" for being anxious or for not trusting God enough is hardly a way forward.

Bonhoeffer proposes another way, which is to become more deeply identified with Jesus Christ, "who has bound his existence to *me*."[4] This means that Christ is not so much with us in our ideal state, but in the messiness of our lives—including when we are anxious. Bonhoeffer goes on to say that "Christ in his being, is *pro me*."[5] In other words, Christ is fundamentally and totally *for* us, even amidst our despair and difficulties.

---

4. Bonhoeffer, *Christ the Center*, 48 (emphasis in original).
5. Bonhoeffer, *Christ the Center*, 47.

A Spirituality of Vulnerability

But this calls us to see Christ more clearly, for he is not the magic "fixer." Bonhoeffer makes the point that "we have seen the exalted one, only as the crucified; the sinless one, only as the guilt-laden; the risen one, as the humiliated." This means that "it is with the humiliated one that the Church goes its own way of humiliation," and it is in this way that the people faith, with all their issues, are to live "in the way of Christ."[6]

In other words, we need to see Christ *with us* in our concerns and anxieties. From that place of identification, who knows what may be spawned in the way of hope, encouragement, and transformation.

> *Lord,*
> *you have always given peace*
> *for the coming day;*
> *and though of anxious heart,*
> *today I believe.*[7]

---

6. Bonhoeffer, *Christ the Center*, 112–13.

7. Northumbria Community, *Celtic Daily Prayer*, 879.

1:2

Identifying with Others

Since there will never cease to be some in need on the earth, I therefore command you, "Open your hand to the poor and neighbor in your land."

—Deuteronomy 15:11

In times of difficulty and distress, particularly when we sense that we have no control over what is happening in our world, it is so easy for us to pull down the shutters and shut others out.

Though Bonhoeffer writes that "sympathy grows in proportion to the fear of approaching disaster,"[8] the reality is that many of us may lose courage and become more self-preoccupied and self-protective. After all, whom can we trust? Is there anyone we can turn to? And who will help us when our *own* needs are so pressing?

The basic message of Scripture, however, points us in another direction. In *all* of life's circumstances, both good and bad, we are called to depend on and trust God—and we are also called to reach out to those in need. Bonhoeffer puts this most clearly: we are to live life "from the perspective of those who suffer."[9]

But how is this possible? And what does this look like?

If our lives have been impacted by Christ, we will seek to follow Christ and be one with Christ, and this oneness binds us to our brothers and sisters in the faith community and also to our neighbor. The very life of Christ moves us towards others. And since Christ gave his life for the whole world (and not simply for those in the church), we must be concerned for all—not simply those in our family or friendship circle.

---

8. Bonhoeffer, *Letters and Papers*, 13.
9. Bonhoeffer, *Letters and Papers*, 17.

A Spirituality of Vulnerability

Bonhoeffer puts this most succinctly, writing that we "must have some share in Christ's large-heartedness"[10] towards others. And while we are to "transform our anxiety . . . into prayers on their behalf," we are also called to "sympathy and action."[11]

All of this may come as a surprise. We may have thought that by embracing salvation in Christ, all would go well with us. But there is much more to the story. For the goodness that we experience in Christ is a goodness that is also meant for others. Bonhoeffer notes that in our "encounter with Christ," we discover that Christ is also "there for others."[12] And so we should be "there for others," too!

Moved by the passion of Christ, we seek to help those who are suffering because we see the hidden face of Christ in their sorrow and pain. And filled with the compassion of Christ, we identify with those who are in need or distress because they remind us of our own vulnerabilities.

Thus our ability to help another does not come from a position of strength, but from the recognition that we have our own needs. When we go out of our way to help someone, we have no way of knowing whether what we have to give will be received. Though we remain open to the possibility that we might be pushed away, we seek to help nonetheless.

Christ has shown us this way of vulnerability, for he gave his life, and yet he was rejected. But in his rejection, he showed us the way home to the very heart of God.

We are to be moved by a similar vision. All of our initiatives to help, whether embraced or rejected, are sacramental acts in the purposes of God—and so we can trust that God will use them for good.

Identifying with others in their need is an act of tenderness, for as Bonhoeffer puts it, we live well by "showing a real sympathy that springs, not from fear, but from the liberating and redeeming love of Christ for all who suffer."[13]

You challenge me to be more generous,
perhaps to share with others
one more thing that I had reserved for my own comfort,
and in relinquishing to find my own healing.[14]

---

10. Bonhoeffer, *Letters and Papers*, 14.
11. Bonhoeffer, *Letters and Papers*, 177, 14.
12. Bonhoeffer, *Letters and Papers*, 381.
13. Bonhoeffer, *Letters and Papers*, 14.
14. Northumbria Community, *Celtic Daily Prayer*, 1129.

1:3

Expectant Listening

*But I have calmed and quieted my soul,
like a weaned child with its mother;
my soul is like the weaned child that is with me.*

—Psalm 131:2

Bonhoeffer lived in deeply troubled times amidst the Nazification of the church, the attack on the Jewish community, the trashing of normal social conventions, and the outbreak of World War II. Before he was imprisoned, he trained clergy for the Confessing Church, which opposed Hitler's ideology, but when he saw the witness of the Confessing Church weakening, he became discouraged.

One could say that Bonhoeffer was exceptionally busy and lived with great pressures to discern the will of God amidst the massive upheavals of his time. He also lived with great grief regarding the compromises that the Confessing Church was willing to make, along with the "death of so many of the best of [his] former pupils."[15]

When we live in extremely difficult times, we can fall into the trap of trying to do more and more, even to the point of exhaustion. While Bonhoeffer faced this, he insists that we cannot "allow ourselves to become so busy that we can't hear God's voice."[16] Rather than abandoning prayer and other spiritual practices, he continued to sustain a life of devotional self-care and openness to God, remaining vulnerable as he sought God's grace, forgiveness, and sustenance.

Bonhoeffer's *Life Together* outlines a brief manual for spiritual practices, but these themes are scattered throughout his writings. He points out that in order to hear God's voice, we need to "open the doors of the heart to

15. Bonhoeffer, *Letters and Papers from Prison*, 215.
16. Bonhoeffer, *Works*, vol. 9, *Young Bonhoeffer, 1918–1927*, 512.

the Master," and "we have to silence all the voices in us."[17] He speaks of the purpose of solitude as "breathing in God's will," "beholding the one who is yearned for," and "yielding to God the right to have the first and last word concerning us."[18] Thus for Bonhoeffer, solitude is not simply a practice of inner piety, but one of listening and embracing the will of God.

Furthermore, Bonhoeffer's writings emphasize that the purpose of solitude is to draw us into repentance as we face the "pain of remorse."[19] Yet when we are "suddenly . . . seized and called to task by the infinite," we need to do so without the fear of "unmasking ourselves."[20] In these passages, we see Bonhoeffer sharing wisdom that was forged in the realities of his life as he encountered God and was transformed by the Spirit.

For Bonhoeffer, solitude was not about coming to a place of emptiness, but rather growing in *expectant listening*. He points out that the most important issue for Christian disciples is to hear "what Jesus Christ himself wants of us," because Christ makes a direct claim on our lives that others do not.[21]

This claim is not, first and foremost, about what we must *do*, but rather who we must *be* and *become*. When the Living Word, Jesus Christ, encounters us, he evokes "whole-hearted faith" in us, which leads us to a commitment "in baptism," where we become "Christ's own possession."[22] As "Christ's possession," we become part of the faith community, the body of Christ—and as part of that community, we are called to be an *incarnational* presence of Christ in the world.

For Bonhoeffer, there is no service without prayer, no contemplation without action, no Sabbath spirituality without daily labor, no being so busy that we neglect friendship with God, no being so involved in the work of justice that we longer have time to drink from the wellsprings of life. Rather, as Bonhoeffer puts it, we are to seek to *be* Christ to the world in *all* that we do. What a call and challenge this is! Thus we need to dig deep wells of life and faith that will sustain us in this calling.

---

17. Bonhoeffer, *Works*, vol. 9, 512.
18. Bonhoeffer, *Works*, vol. 10, *Barcelona, Berlin, New York 1928–1931*, 502–4.
19. Bonhoeffer, *Works*, vol. 10, 502.
20. Bonhoeffer, *Works*, vol. 10, 503–4.
21. Bonhoeffer, *Cost of Discipleship*, 29, 86.
22. Bonhoeffer, *Cost of Discipleship*, 203, 206.

*Evening comes when You call,
and all nature listens to You
because You hold it all.
And now You hold me.*[23]

---

[23]. Northumbria Community, *Celtic Daily Prayer,* 1049.

1:4

Praying Through Difficulties

About that time King Herod laid violent hands upon some who belonged to the church. He had James . . . killed with the sword . . . [and] proceeded to arrest Peter also. While Peter was kept in prison, the church prayed fervently to God for him.

—Acts 12:1–5

Bonhoeffer seemed certain that troubled times would lead us to prayer, writing, "it's true that it needs trouble to shake us up and drive us to prayer."[24] But he acknowledges that he is ashamed of this fact, for he wrote these words when "bombs [were] falling . . . all around the [prison]."[25]

And he may well be right. Times of difficulty may stop us in our tracks. We may seriously re-evaluate some aspects of our lives and conclude that we have been blind or foolish about certain things. We may come to the "blinding" realization that we have lived life far too unreflectively. And we may even acknowledge that we have been far too self-sufficient and lacking in prayer.

But troubled times may also have the opposite effect. We may become more reactive, angry, and disillusioned. We may even believe that God has lost interest in our lives and world and has abandoned us.

Times of difficulty are not a single road to something better. They do not carry clear messages, but are more like a murky lake. In this intermediate zone, things often feel topsy-turvy, and we may well find ourselves heading into a tailspin.

Thus our first move in times of crisis and difficulty must be to *stop and to be still* and *reflective* rather than to react. Our opening prayers in these seasons can be, "God, what are you saying in these circumstances? What is your invitation? What are you calling me to be and to do?"

24. Bonhoeffer, *Letters and Papers*, 199.
25. Bonhoeffer, *Letters and Papers*, 199.

Such prayers are more to the point than prayers of reaction or self-pity. It's so easy to blame God or others. It's so easy to pray, "Why me?" But these prayers push God away instead of inviting God into the very center of our feelings and circumstances.

I believe that difficulties say much more to us than we might think. They speak to us of a good but flawed world, of happy days and disasters, of blessings and difficulties. But they also speak to us of a God who does not magically protect us—a God who is loving and caring, but has also given us freedom. This means that times of crisis may open up all sorts of questions and issues, including those of our faith.

In other words, difficulties speak to us about the complexities and messiness of life, and they open up the many issues of our faith for which we don't have nice and easy answers. During these times, we are not invited to live the answers, but to live the *questions*.[26]

Bonhoeffer may well be right in his observation that during times of difficulty, things that we normally take for granted are shaken, and so we cry out to God for answers.

Where Bonhoeffer takes us regarding these pressing matters is most unexpected. Instead of pressing us to pray more and to be more pious, he points us in another direction. He says that the call to be a disciple of Jesus Christ does not land us in a place of safety and certainty, but rather in a "life of absolute insecurity," because in "adherence to the person of Jesus," we are called to "endure the cross," which is "laid on every Christian."[27]

What this means is that we don't simply pray because of a crisis. Rather, since the whole of our life in following Jesus is marked by faith in the face of uncertainty, our whole life becomes a prayer. Living in this precarious way, yet ever linked with Christ, is a "holy life," according to Bonhoeffer, and this life is a "prayer of love."[28]

Saying prayers is one thing. *Being* prayer is something else altogether.

> *The God of life with guarding hold you;*
> *the loving Christ with guarding fold you;*
> *the Holy Spirit guarding, mould you;*
> *each night of life to aid, enfold you;*
> *each day and night of life uphold you.*[29]

---

26. Rilke speaks of living the questions in *Letters to a Young Poet*, 35.
27. Bonhoeffer, *Cost of Discipleship*, 49, 77, 79.
28. Bonhoeffer, *Cost of Discipleship*, 136.
29. Northumbria Community, *Celtic Daily Prayer*, 945.

1:5

Following the "Hidden" Christ

Jesus began to show his disciples that he must go to Jerusalem and undergo great suffering . . . , be killed, and on the third day be raised. And Peter took him aside and began to rebuke him, saying, . . . "This must never happen to you." But he turned and said to Peter, "Get behind me, Satan! You are a stumbling-block to me; for you are setting your mind not on divine things but on human things."

—MATTHEW 16:21–23

Peter assumed that he had worked out what it meant to follow Jesus. He thought he knew what the person and mission of Jesus was all about. But he was wrong. He had misunderstood.

And we can so easily do the same, particularly in our present-day culture, where we have become the center of the world and everything is simply about us. In this frame, we can see Jesus as someone who is there simply to benefit *us*.

We in the West have distorted so much of the gospel story. Thankfully, we can learn from Bonhoeffer, who saw Jesus in a very different light.

First, Bonhoeffer stresses that Christ is the "Word in the form of a living address" to humanity, which includes both the word of "forgiveness" as well as the "command" to "assume responsibility."[30] Our great calling is to *be* Christ to the world.

But Bonhoeffer also points out that in the preaching of the church, Christ as Word is present in "hidden form."[31] What he means is that Christ is only discernible with the eyes of faith, and he is both a contradiction and

---

30. Bonhoeffer, *Christ the Center*, 50–51.
31. Bonhoeffer, *Christ the Center*, 46.

a "stumbling block."³² So much of the way of Christ is strange to us. His gospel has an unusual, counterintuitive melody.

Second, Bonhoeffer notes that in the Eucharist, we partake of the mystery of Christ, the "embodied Word," who is present in the sacrament both in his "exaltation" as the risen Lord who is with us, but also in his "humiliation" in the bread and wine.³³ Surely, we often look in the wrong places to find the One who is so hidden and lowly!

Third, and even more disconcertingly, Bonhoeffer believes that Christ exists as fellowship, which he describes as "Christ *as* Church."³⁴ Because the faith community receives "the Word of revelation," which is Christ, the church is an embodiment of Christ.³⁵

Yet here also Bonhoeffer stresses the challenge of seeing Christ in both his exaltation and the humiliation of his body. Bonhoeffer certainly did not idealize the church, for he writes of a time of "utter decline and breakdown" and the "creaking and groaning of church structures."³⁶ He further observes that saints "are aware of the weakness and sin in their lives" and "remain justified sinners."³⁷ Thus Christ is often hidden in the church and needs to be discerned with a heart of love.

Finally, Bonhoeffer sees Christ as the "hidden center" of "human nature, existence, of history, and of creation,"³⁸ because *all* humans are created in the image of God and are fully provided for in the redemptive work of Christ. Through the Word, the Spirit, and the witness of the faith community, Christ dwells *in* the world, and "the whole of human existence" is his domain and is "the beginning of the new world of God."³⁹

This means that no domain of life exists outside the presence and influence of Christ. Yet no domain, including the faith community, is without idolatry. Thus everywhere, everyone is called to ongoing faith, conversion, repentance, and discernment.

To see Christ in a culturally captive church, a dictatorial state, a dysfunctional society, or broken families and individual lives is a way of *seeing*

---

32. Bonhoeffer, *Christ the Center*, 46.
33. Bonhoeffer, *Christ the Center*, 46, 53, 57.
34. Bonhoeffer, *Christ the Center*, 46, 58 (emphasis in original).
35. Bonhoeffer, *Christ the Center*, 58.
36. Bonhoeffer, *Works*, vol. 12, *Berlin 1932–1933*, 459, 477.
37. Bonhoeffer, *Cost of Discipleship*, 257, 250.
38. Bonhoeffer, *Christ the Center*, 62, 60.
39. Bonhoeffer, *Christ the Center*, 65.

A Spirituality of Vulnerability

anew, well beyond rationality. From this new perspective, *we see in the spasms of the present world the agitation and gestation of the kingdom of God.* Such seeing requires our minds to be shaped by the grand redemptive story of Scripture, our hearts to be softened by the love of Christ, and our eyes to behold what is yet to unfold in our time by the grace and goodness of God.

While we may think that we have Christ all worked out, we are in for continual surprises. He may well appear where we least expect him!

> *Of this I am certain.*
> *All the rest, emotions, enthusiasm, and desires*
> *are not in themselves grace,*
> *only the tokens of grace.*
> *And these [God] may often withdraw,*
> *sometimes to strengthen our patience . . .*
> *but always for our spiritual good though we may never understand.*[40]

---

40. From *The Cloud of Unknowing* (fourteenth century). Quoted in Ringma and Alexander, eds., *Of Martyrs, Monks, and Mystics*, 67.

1:6

Facing Disappointment

Barnabas wanted to take with them John called Mark. But Paul decided not to take with them one who had deserted them . . . and had not accompanied them in the work. The disagreement became so sharp that they parted company.

—Acts 15:37–39

There is nothing more precarious than to start a new project. After much wrestling, Bonhoeffer and other colleagues finally came to the conclusion that they could no longer serve a church that was committed to Nazi ideology, but needed to start a new church.

What a project and challenge! And all the more, since most Christian leaders and their congregations supported the church under Hitler's influence.

Starting something new requires a careful analysis of the old with all its defects. The envisaged new may need a completely new foundation. At the same time, the vision needs to be credible and doable rather than some idealistic dream.

Bonhoeffer worked hard in the formation of this new Confessing Church, especially in the training of clergy. In a "Letter to the Finkenwalde Brothers" in 1937, he recounts to his students how they "had found the church of Jesus Christ" and "actually experienced it," the church "that follows the Lord under the cross" and is "obedient solely" to Christ.[41]

But all of this was very short-lived. The seminary was soon closed by the Gestapo. Many students were conscripted into the army as chaplains. And the church leadership failed to chart a clear way forward in opposing Hitler's ongoing attacks on the Confessing Church.

---

41. Bonhoeffer, *Works*, vol. 15, *Theological Education Underground 1937–1940*, 29, 35, 30.

A Spirituality of Vulnerability

Throughout Bonhoeffer's writings at this time, he vents his disappointment. He realizes that everyone is not clear about "how much personal sacrifice" will be required.[42] He laments that the Confessing Church has "lost its faith-awakening and . . . its discerning power."[43] And he points out that many have failed to see that "God's cause is not always the cause of success."[44] Bonhoeffer points to the "failure of church leadership," but he acknowledges that "hearts and hands . . . are tired."[45]

Since experiencing disappointment is not restricted to Bonhoeffer, but is very much a part of Christian service, we need to draw some lessons from these headwinds in the Christian life. Disappointments and spirituality are not unrelated, but we need to discover their complementarity. For disappointments can purge, renew, and revitalize our spirituality, and this renewed spirituality can sustain us through times of ongoing disappointment.

Disappointments come to all of us and call us to perseverance. In such circumstances, we may need to pray for faithfulness and forgiveness, particularly in forgiving those who have disappointed us. But we may also need to pray for forgiveness for ourselves as we may be the source of certain disappointments.

Disappointments can also be a factor in changing us. For as Bonhoeffer acknowledges, "it needs trouble to shake up and drive us to prayer."[46] Moreover, "sympathy grows in proportion to the fear of approaching disaster."[47]

Yet disappointments can serve as a turning point—not only to greater fidelity in times of difficulty, but also towards something new. Disappointments are therefore an invitation to review what we have committed our lives to and then to discern a new sense of direction.

As Bonhoeffer saw the Confessing Church being undermined, both internally and externally, he began to think about other ways to resist the damage that Hitler was doing to the church, Germany, and the world. This led to his controversial involvement with the *Abwehr* and his being implicated in its attempts on Hitler's life.

---

42. Bonhoeffer, *Works*, vol. 15, 30.
43. Bonhoeffer, *Works*, vol. 15, 31.
44. Bonhoeffer, *Works*, vol. 15, 82.
45. Bonhoeffer, *Works*, vol. 15, 417–18.
46. Bonhoeffer, *Letters and Papers*, 199.
47. Bonhoeffer, *Letters and Papers*, 13.

The challenge here is that disappointments call us to careful re-evaluation—and because disappointment is a regular part of life, we will face this challenge continually!

> *I had hoped for different outcomes.*
> *I had hoped for different opportunities.*
> *I did not expect what I had worked hard to secure*
> *would be dismantled*
> *far beyond my control.*
> *My life is Yours. You know my heart.*[48]

---

48. Northumbria Community, *Celtic Daily Prayer*, 1122–23.

2

A Spirituality of Joining

Introduction

WHILE MUCH OF THE pull in daily life may be towards fragmentation and individualism, this movement scatters rather than builds. Our challenge is to move toward joining, community, mutuality, and reciprocity.

These concepts are easy to say, but much harder to do! There are also dangers, as we might end up joining a cause, ideology, or movement that is cultic in orientation, promising much but delivering forms of bondage.

This threat leaves us with many questions about what healthy joining and community look like. Several factors stand out. First, joining needs to be free of compulsion and manipulation. Second, whatever movement or cause we join needs to maintain a healthy balance of corporate leadership, member participation, accountability structures, and credible goals for its purpose and mission. Third, there needs to be clear understanding about individual needs and responsibilities as well as communal structures and demands.

Within a Christian frame, joining has a wonderful dialectic. In Christ, through the Spirit, we join in the presence and purposes of God. This "being in Christ"—a major theme in the Pauline writings—both "binds" us to Christ and frees us to become who we are truly meant to be. We are freed from our "false" self to become our "true" self, and our life's purpose shifts from the burden of our own self-efforts to living in dependence on the grace and love of God. Our joining is also relationally dynamic and faith-oriented, which leads us to various spiritual practices that can enhance the relationship we have in Christ.

But the joining mosaic is even richer and more colorful, for being "bound" to Christ also means being "connected" to our brothers and sisters in the faith community. In this community of word, sacraments, fellowship, and service, we build each other up in following Christ, and we also learn to help and serve each other as if we are serving Christ himself. This community is a second "incarnation" and demonstrates to the world something of who Christ is and what Christ has done in providing restoration for the whole world.

For we are not only joined to the faith community, but also to the wider world. We see *all* others as made in God's image and provided for in Christ's salvation. And we seek to join with all others in making our world more sustainable, peaceful, and just. Most simply put, when we seek to live "in Christ," we join in the dance of love of God and love of neighbor.

Amidst the great challenges of Bonhoeffer's time, he discerned whom to join in building an opposition movement to Hitler's madness—and also whom to resist. Building what is good and just in a time of tyranny and war is no easy task, for any attempts at resistance will be marked by opposition and suspicion and characterized by fragility and vulnerability. But above all, such attempts are marked by faith in the God who journeys with us in dark times, along with the courage that is spawned when hands are joined in the common cause of righteousness.

The move towards joining involves the art of discernment, for there can be powerful forces trying to coerce us into joining a wrong cause or to dissuade us from joining a just cause. And as Bonhoeffer and others who have faced opposition know, the work of joining may cost our life.

2:1

Living in Christ

So if anyone is in Christ, there is a new creation: everything old has passed away; see, everything has become new!

—2 CORINTHIANS 5:17

Even though Bonhoeffer knew very early in his life that he wanted to be a theologian, and he completed his theological doctoral studies in his early twenties, he writes: "I discovered the Bible . . . but I had not yet become a Christian."[1] Later, he confesses that the Sermon on the Mount "freed" him from turning the word of God to his own advantage, for he experienced "a great liberation."[2]

Bonhoeffer's ongoing wrestling with what it meant to be joined to Christ in discipleship eventually led to his death. One could say that Christ became Bonhoeffer's center point, out of which he lived his life through the most difficult circumstances. Yet Christ was not merely a comfort to Bonhoeffer amidst the agonies of Hitler's Germany, nor only a hope in Bonhoeffer's anticipation of God's final future. Rather, Christ was a *present sustenance* and *empowerment* in Bonhoeffer's task of prophetic witness.

Bonhoeffer had a profound sense that Jesus was not just a figure of the historical past, a story in an ancient book, a moral ideal, or a utopian guru. Instead, Bonhoeffer saw Christ as God incarnate and present in word, sacrament, and community—one who is "hidden" in the midst of the world.

He notes that "Jesus is the Christ present as the Crucified and as the Risen One," who in freedom has "bound his existence to me."[3] Moreover, he writes that Christ is the head of "the new humanity."[4]

---

1. Quoted in Bethge, *Dietrich Bonhoeffer*, 205.
2. Quoted in Bethge, *Dietrich Bonhoeffer*, 205.
3. Bonhoeffer, *Christ the Center*, 43, 48.
4. Bonhoeffer, *Christ the Center*, 48.

In *The Cost of Discipleship*, Bonhoeffer sets out what it means to be joined to Christ as a disciple. On the one hand, he writes that "only the sufferings of Christ are a means of atonement" and that there is "redemptive efficacy" in Christ's sufferings.[5] On the other hand, he stresses that we are bound in "allegiance to the suffering Christ."[6] Bonhoeffer further explains that discipleship, which is at the heart of being joined to Christ, calls us to an "adherence to the person of Jesus," which necessarily means that "the 'must' of suffering applies to his disciples."[7]

This has profound meanings for us today. For Bonhoeffer did not see his being joined to Christ primarily as a source of benefits, but rather as a source of a radical identification. Joined to Christ, Bonhoeffer believed that he was called to seek to *be* Christ to the world.

At the same time, Bonhoeffer did not see his attachment to Christ simply as a guarantee of future bliss, but rather as the source of his profound engagement in the issues and challenges of his time. From Bonhoeffer's perspective, we cannot follow an escapist theology, nor a prosperity gospel, as both these place the human being at the center.

Rather, Bonhoeffer sees that in the incarnation of Jesus Christ—in his way of life, his death, and his resurrection—we have the inspirational center for what a renewed humanity and world can look like.

This means that when we join with Christ, we are called to be *like* Christ, and thus we will seek to do what he did by entering into his purposes for humanity. In joining with Christ, we both gain new life in Christ and, at the same time, we give away our life for the sake of the reign of God, who comes amongst us to inspire and to heal.

As you grow
may faith grow with you.
May you find the presence of Christ
your clothing and protection.
And year by year
may the knowledge of His presence be greater for you,
that daily you may put on Christ and walk as His own
in the world.[8]

---

5. Bonhoeffer, *Cost of Discipleship*, 79, 82.
6. Bonhoeffer, *Cost of Discipleship*, 80.
7. Bonhoeffer, *Cost of Discipleship*, 77.
8. Northumbria Community, *Celtic Daily Prayer*, 206.

A Spirituality of Joining

2:2

Joining the Suffering Christ

But rejoice insofar as you are sharing Christ's sufferings, so that you may also be glad and shout for joy when his glory is revealed.

—1 Peter 4:13

During Bonhoeffer's days of insecurity and turmoil, amidst the abuses of political power and the compromise of the church, it would have been tempting for him to try to solve problems by seeking to implement an impregnable agenda. In formulating that agenda, it would have been tempting to try to cast Christ and the Christian message in watertight terms.

Even in our day, some Christians living in Majority World dictatorships seek political office so that they can serve as "benevolent" dictators. And globally, many Christians have become enamored with the "prosperity" gospel. In other words, Christians across cultures and time have tried to seek power in order to "do good." But those who hold these aspirations often lack a sound Christology and an adequate understanding of the nature of power.

Once again, Bonhoeffer can come to our aid. But first, we should note how strange it is to talk about joining the suffering Christ, for surely we all want to join a winner and be part of a winning team. This raises the question, isn't Christ a winner?

But Christ is strangely different from the successful person we would like him to be. Though he is the icon of the new humanity, he forces no one. Though he is the redeemer of the whole world, not everyone embraces his healing gifts. Though he is the crucified and risen Lord, not all are impressed with his ways. And while Christians in faith see Christ as the Lord of history, much of Christ's ways remain "hidden" in the world, because the way of Christ and his life-giving reign exist provisionally through the work of the Spirit and are still awaiting their full manifestation.

Bonhoeffer puts this most clearly: "we have seen the exalted one, only as the crucified; the sinless one, only as the guilt-laden; the risen one, only as the humiliated."[9] Moreover, "it is with this humiliated one that the church goes its own way of humiliation."[10]

This means that when we join with Christ, we are not joining a winner from the world's perspective. Instead, we are joining a most enigmatic figure whose way in the world seems to be one of loss in order to gain—and in whose death lies resurrection power.

In seeking to understand this enigmatic Christ and what it means to join him in his way of being in the world, Bonhoeffer turned to the Sermon on the Mount, particularly the Beatitudes. In these challenging teachings of Jesus, we find the *magna carta* of our earthly sojourn and citizenship, with all its precarity and challenges. There is nothing powerful here in earthly terms—only the strength and goodness of vulnerability.

In the Beatitudes, the "pure in heart," according to Bonhoeffer, are those who "renounce their own good" in order to "rely solely upon Jesus."[11] They are "meek" because they "renounce every right of their own" and recognize that their only right is "the will of their Lord."[12]

In this relationship, those who seek the way of Jesus are never fully settled, for they long to keep growing and are always on the road. As Bonhoeffer puts it, "those who follow Jesus grow hungry and thirsty on the way," even though they long "for complete renewal."[13]

In their identification with the suffering Christ, they "mourn for the world, for its guilt, for its fate, and its fortune," and so they "take upon themselves the distress and humiliation and sin of others," and they "renounce all violence" and "endure suffering."[14]

Christians who identify with Christ in this way are not seeking to live in a "holy bubble," untouched by their surroundings. Rather, while living in Christ and seeking the way of Christ, they are marked by the grace of Christ as they embrace the challenge to live more fully in the reign of God. At the same time, they are always willing to suffer on behalf of the world, for they desire that Christ may be reborn in the woundedness of our world.

9. Bonhoeffer, *Christ the Center*, 112.
10. Bonhoeffer, *Christ the Center*, 113.
11. Bonhoeffer, *Cost of Discipleship*, 101.
12. Bonhoeffer, *Cost of Discipleship*, 99.
13. Bonhoeffer, *Cost of Discipleship*, 100.
14. Bonhoeffer, *Cost of Discipleship*, 98, 100, 102.

A Spirituality of Joining

*If I open my eyes to the world around me,
if I open my heart to the people that surround me,
then I feel pain and brokenness,
I see suffering and injustice.
Deliver us, Lord, from every evil
and grant us peace in our day,
in your mercy, Lord.*[15]

---

15. Northumbria Community, *Celtic Daily Prayer*, 159.

2:3

Joining the Suffering Church

For in the one Spirit we were all baptized into one body—Jews or Greeks, slaves or free—and we were all made to drink of one Spirit.

—1 Corinthians 12:13

Because Bonhoeffer was so concerned with the person and work of Christ, he was also concerned about the nature and function of the church. He believed that Christology had everything to do with ecclesiology, which meant that the faithful church must reflect its attachment to Christ. This understanding was particularly pressing in his time, as the church was being shaped by Nazi ideology.

Bonhoeffer recognized the momentous nature of the struggle in front of him, for it was not only about the future of the church in Germany, but the "existence of Christianity in Europe."[16]

In response, Bonhoeffer tackled the Aryan clause, which stated that Jews could no longer hold an office in the church. He also rejected the Führer principle, which promoted a "political-messianic" leader, to whom "the individual surrenders ultimate responsibility."[17] And together with others, he came to the conclusion that a new church, the Confessing Church, must come into being.

He believed that this church must be a discipleship community, where the members would be freed from their old existence by being bound "to Jesus Christ alone."[18] And wherever this faith in Christ came to expression, he believed there would be "obedience"[19] in living the Sermon on the Mount.

---

16. Bonhoeffer, *Works*, vol., 13, *London 1933–1935*, 118.
17. Bonhoeffer, *Works*, vol. 12, *Berlin 1932–1933*, 459, 278, 277.
18. Bonhoeffer, *Cost of Discipleship*, 53.
19. Bonhoeffer, *Cost of Discipleship*, 54.

A Spirituality of Joining

Bonhoeffer identified the faith community as a sign, witness, and radical insertion of Christ's presence in the world. Thus he believed that the church was tasked with calling the world to its true destiny and its full incorporation into the salvific work of Christ. Moreover, he believed that the faith community was called to share life together in order to reflect and be Christ to one another for the sake of the world.

This robust ecclesiology stands in sharp contrast to the present-day church, particularly in the West, where the church has largely become a moribund institution that is culturally captive to contemporary culture. Rather than seeing this as unfortunate or simply "the way it is," Bonhoeffer would challenge us to confront this disfigurement of the faith community.

Many Christians are facing this challenge with suggestions about how the church can improve—either in the form of multiple small communities,[20] or by living in the power of the Spirit,[21] or by becoming a missional church,[22] an emergent church,[23] a lay church,[24] or a slow church,[25] among others.

Bonhoeffer, however, points us in a different direction. He believes that we need to recover a deeper Christology, which will lead to a renewed vision of the church. This Christology has at its heart a Christo-mysticism, where Christ, through the Spirit, is present in preaching, in the sacraments, and through the fellowship of the faith community. He emphasizes the presence of Christ in spiritual practices and in every dimension of the church's life. The fundamental issue is not what the church is to *do*, but who it *is* in the purposes of God.

In this emphasis, Bonhoeffer is not promoting a triumphalistic church, but a suffering church that is following the suffering Messiah. And joining such a church is an act of humiliation, for we are not only called to serve others in the faith community, but also "to bear the sins of others" and to act in a "vicarious" capacity in relation to the sins and brokenness of our world.[26]

In our age, which is shaped by image, success, and utilitarianism, Bonhoeffer challenges the church to live as a vulnerable community that is

---

20. Rahner, *Shape of the Church to Come.*
21. Moltmann, *Church in the Power of the Spirit.*
22. Guder, ed., *Missional Church.*
23. McLaren, *Generous Orthodoxy.*
24. Stevens, *Liberating the Laity.*
25. Smith and Pattison, *Slow Church.*
26. Bonhoeffer, *Cost of Discipleship*, 80, 220.

seeking to live *in* Christ and in the *way* of the suffering Christ on behalf of the world. We may well find this an impossible challenge, but we are called to serve others as if we are serving Christ himself.

> *Father, I abandon myself into your hands.*
> *Do with me what you will.*
> *Whatever you do, I will thank you.*
> *I am ready for all, I accept all.*
> *Let only your will be done in me, as in all your creatures.*
> *And I will ask nothing else, my Lord.*[27]

---

27. Northumbria Community, *Celtic Daily Prayer*, 49.

2:4

Joining the Suffering of the World

"But I say to you that listen, Love your enemies, do good to those who hate you, bless those who curse you, pray for those who abuse you."

—Luke 6:27–28

It is not easy to be concerned about others—especially when living through difficult and oppressive circumstances.

Bonhoeffer was surrounded by immense difficulties—the Nazi regime, the compromised church, the shutdown of the seminary for the new Confessing Church, the failure to get support from foreign church leaders, and his own imprisonment, which separated him from the woman he loved.

In such circumstances, it would be easy to question God and sink into despair, to abandon God and think only about oneself. Yet even though Bonhoeffer struggled, he did not succumb to these temptations.

His writings reveal that he experienced temptation, for he recognizes that one can be tempted to believe "that God had deserted them," and he acknowledges that this belief "leads the believer into the deepest loneliness."[28]

But he also notes that temptation can facilitate a "turning to God" and a "strengthening of faith" so that one can "experience the sufferings of this world."[29] In other words, no matter the extent of one's difficulties, it is always possible to relate to and be available for others.

In identifying with Christ and the faith community, Bonhoeffer never sought escapism, for he had a deep concern for the human community and his country. He saw the call to prayer as a way of joining in the human community, and he emphasized that the hidden work of the faith community was "to intercede for the world."[30]

---

28. Bonhoeffer, *Works*, vol. 15, *Theological Education Underground 1937–1940*, 412, 413.
29. Bonhoeffer, *Works*, vol. 15, 407.
30. Bonhoeffer, *Works*, vol. 15, 327.

Moreover, he writes that "there is no community with Jesus that is not at the same time *a call to service.*"[31] This call raises a challenging question for us today.

So many of us in the contemporary world are so focused on our own issues and concerns that our service to others involves an occasional prayer and a donation to some charity. Others may be concerned about living as salt and light for the sake of the kingdom of God in our respective workplaces and neighborhoods. And others may have a vision to volunteer in some missional capacity, either at home or abroad.

But Bonhoeffer sees the call to join and serve the human community in a much deeper way. First, he identifies our fundamental connection to one another, since all humans are made in the image of God. Second, he recognizes that all of us have been impacted by Christ's salvific work and the significance of the incarnation. Third, he notes that in "Jesus Christ the reality of God entered into the reality of this world," and therefore the *world does not exist* "independently of the revelation of God in Christ."[32]

Observing that Christ "stands between us and God" and that those who are in Christ stand between the world and God, he extends this insight even further by asserting that the Christian "has to bear the sins of others" and, as a "scapegoat," be willing to "bear their shame."[33]

Rather than being unconcerned about the world, Bonhoeffer calls Christians to be so concerned that they are willing to take "vicarious representative action."[34] This action has many dimensions, which include prayer for the world, prophetic witness regarding the world's idolatries, serving those affected by society's wrongdoing, and vicarious suffering.

Bonhoeffer's life exemplified this profound sense of joining with Christ as he engaged the troubles of his time. If we are going to walk a similar road in our age, we will need to find deep inner resources.

> *You must comfort the sick*
> *And yet have nothing for yourself,*
> *You must drink the water of suffering*
> *And light the fire of love with the wood of virtues.*
> *Thus, you live in the true desert.*[35]

---

31. Bonhoeffer, *Works*, vol. 15, 544 (emphasis in original).
32. Bonhoeffer, *Ethics*, 192, 195.
33. Bonhoeffer, *Cost of Discipleship*, 85, 80.
34. Bonhoeffer, *Works*, vol. 1, *Sanctorum Communio*, 120.
35. From Mechthild of Magdeburg (c. 1120–1280). Quoted in Ringma and Alexander,

2:5

Joining the Poor

I know that the Lord maintains the cause of the needy,
and executes justice for the poor.

—PSALM 140:12

The category of the poor needs to be understood in very comprehensive terms. The poor are not only those who are at the bottom of the ladder of social stratification. More broadly, they are all those who have been sinned against and marginalized.

Bonhoeffer clearly demonstrated a heart for the poor. He did so early in his ministry by serving working-class youth, later in his support of the Jews amidst Hitler's racial madness, and in the final years of his life in his service to fellow prisoners.

In the early days of the Nazi regime, Bonhoeffer rejected Hitler's attempt to exclude Jews from leadership roles in the church. He went on to propose that the church has the right to question the state and "to accuse the state of offenses against morality."[36] Furthermore, Bonhoeffer stressed that the church should provide help "to the victims of state's actions."[37] Finally, Bonhoeffer made a most controversial statement, writing that when Christians help those who are sinned against, they should act "not to just bind up the wounds of the victims beneath the wheel, but to seize the wheel itself."[38] Here he is speaking of taking more direct action to resist the oppressors.

Eberhard Bethge, Bonhoeffer's student, confidant, and biographer, notes that Bonhoeffer's Tegel prison experience was a "'borderline'

---

eds., *Of Martyrs, Monks, and Mystics*, 226.

36. Bonhoeffer, *Works*, vol. 12, *Berlin 1932–1933*, 363.
37. Bonhoeffer, *Works*, vol. 12, 365.
38. Bonhoeffer, *Works*, vol. 12, 365.

situation."[39] What he meant was that Bonhoeffer had good relationships with some of the guards, who provided "small favors"[40] for him. But Bonhoeffer used these favors to help his fellow prisoners. He wrote a report to improve prison conditions. He arranged for prisoners' families to get help from his parents, including legal assistance. And he provided moral and spiritual support for his inmates, including writing prayers for them.[41] Bethge concludes that along with the other prisoners, Bonhoeffer "shared their anxieties, privations, and little joys."[42]

Bonhoeffer's theological reflections on serving the poor express the heartbeat of the Christian life, which is that the "love of God and love for one's human neighbor are indissolubly united."[43] But he grounds this theological conviction christologically, writing that in Christ, "God became a poor, wretched, unknown, unsuccessful human being."[44] Therefore, all who seek to be like Christ and carry his vision into the world "cannot get away . . . from the world,"[45] which includes the poor and those who have been sinned against.

In *The Cost of Discipleship*, Bonhoeffer notes that "the incarnation is the ultimate reason why the service of God cannot be divorced from the service" of others.[46] He goes on to highlight the generous scope of Christ's salvific work, writing that Jesus "suffered for the sake of all his people," and therefore we should do the same. Then Bonhoeffer asks a pointed question: who "will come forward to help him and work with him?"[47]

Though Christ's redemptive work has all in view, the faith community is called to be especially attentive to the poor and needy because it is so easy to neglect them. Bonhoeffer stresses that the community in Christ is "the new fellowship of brotherly [and sisterly] living," which manifests a whole new way of life.[48] In casting a vision for this way of life, he observes that "where the world oppresses," Christians "will stoop down and raise

39. Bethge, *Dietrich Bonhoeffer*, 841.
40. Bethge, *Dietrich Bonhoeffer*, 848.
41. Bethge, *Dietrich Bonhoeffer*, 849–50.
42. Bethge, *Dietrich Bonhoeffer*, 853.
43. Bonhoeffer, *Works*, vol. 15, *Theological Education Underground 1937–1940*, 112.
44. Bonhoeffer, *Works*, vol. 15, 112.
45. Bonhoeffer, *Works*, vol. 15, 112.
46. Bonhoeffer, *Cost of Discipleship*, 117.
47. Bonhoeffer, *Cost of Discipleship*, 179, 181.
48. Bonhoeffer, *Cost of Discipleship*, 232.

up the oppressed."[49] Moreover, he reveals his compassion for those who have been sinned against by calling all Christians to "share in Christ's largeheartedness" by demonstrating "a real sympathy that springs not from fear, but from the liberating and redeeming love of Christ for all who suffer."[50]

For Bonhoeffer, our Christian call is clear. Because "God stoops down in Jesus Christ," even to the depths of human "downfall, of guilt, and misery," we are all called to respond to "the hungry . . . [person who] needs bread, and the homeless . . . [person who] needs a roof, the dispossessed . . . [person who] needs justice, and the lonely . . . [person who] needs fellowship, the undisciplined [person who] needs order, and the slave [who] needs freedom."[51]

> *How dare you wrap God up as good behavior*
> *and tell the poor*
> *that they should be like you?*
> *How can you live at ease*
> *with riches and success*
> *while those I love go hungry and are oppressed?*
> *It really is for such a time as this*
> *that I was given breath.*[52]

---

49. Bonhoeffer, *Cost of Discipleship*, 232.
50. Bonhoeffer, *Letters and Papers*, 14.
51. Bonhoeffer, *Ethics*, 136.
52. Northumbria Community, *Celtic Daily Prayer*, 200.

2:6

Joining God's Kingdom Purposes

"The Spirit of the Lord is upon me,
because he has anointed me
to bring good news to the poor.
He has sent me to proclaim release to the captives
and recovery of sight to the blind,
to let the oppressed go free,
to proclaim the year of the Lord's favor."

—LUKE 4:18–19

In Bonhoeffer's works, he emphasizes that the church should live as a second "incarnation" of Christ, carrying on the salvific work of Christ and the dynamics of the reign of God. In emphasizing the reign of God, he was confronting Hitler's formation of a political "kingdom" based on racism, oppression, and the violation of human rights.

Bonhoeffer knew that Hitler's utopian, demonic vision could never be resisted by simply calling Christians to foster an inner piety and pray more. Although Bonhoeffer affirmed the need to "build . . . a strong fortress within" so that one would be secure in God,[53] he understood that there needed to be a much greater Christian response to Hitler's Third Reich.

Thus Bonhoeffer stresses that "belonging wholly to Christ" is central to the Christian life, and he also insists that the Christian "stands at the same time wholly in the world"—including the political realm.[54] Moreover, he argues that the task of the faith community is to proclaim to the whole world and to every aspect of life that "the world . . . [is] loved by God and

---

53. Bonhoeffer, *Works*, vol. 12, *Berlin 1932–1933*, 287.
54. Bonhoeffer, *Ethics*, 198.

reconciled with Him."⁵⁵ Because the world cannot exist "independently of the revelation of God in Christ,"⁵⁶ we are to live *every* aspect of life under the Lordship of God.

If we are to live every aspect of life under the Lordship of God, then the political realm can never be a self-existing, self-justifying realm, because God is Lord of both the ecclesiastical and the secular realms. In the former, God is openly acknowledged, but in the latter, God is a hidden presence. Bonhoeffer believed that Christians are called to live their faith in both realms—and he understood that Christian spirituality would have to be robust enough to sustain us in every domain of life.

Yet Bonhoeffer perceived that Christians would always be "susceptible to the religion of otherworldliness" because of their conservatism and weakness, and he knew that this false religion would cause them to turn a blind eye to the challenges and idolatries of their time. At the same time, Bonhoeffer believed that Christ could make us strong if we would embrace his call to love the earth "as God's earth" and to love the kingdom of God as "*God's kingdom on earth.*"⁵⁷ Moreover, he believed that those "who love the Earth and God as one, can believe in God's kingdom."⁵⁸

Bonhoeffer makes it quite clear in his writing that the kingdom of God is not about the "strengthening of the church," nor the "Christianizing of culture and politics," nor the "renewal of Christian moral convention."⁵⁹ In other words, *we* cannot build the kingdom of God because the reign of God is not *our* project!

Rather, as Bonhoeffer puts it, the kingdom of God "is miraculous" and "comes to us" as a "*kingdom of resurrection*"—for "where God is, there is God's kingdom."⁶⁰

Bonhoeffer concludes that the kingdom is always like hidden treasure, and when we pray for the kingdom to come, this binds the church "to the Earth" in all its misery and need.⁶¹

---

55. Bonhoeffer, *Ethics*, 200.
56. Bonhoeffer, *Ethics*, 195.
57. Bonhoeffer, *Works*, vol. 12, *Berlin 1932–1933*, 286, 288 (emphasis in original).
58. Bonhoeffer, *Works*, vol. 12, 286.
59. Bonhoeffer, *Works*, vol. 12, 291.
60. Bonhoeffer, *Works*, vol. 12, 292.
61. Bonhoeffer, *Works*, vol. 12, 289.

A spirituality that is focused on the coming reign of God beckons us to prayer, draws us to God, calls us to fidelity in the faith community, and plunges us into the world to seek its healing and transformation.

> *Our Father, who art in heaven,*
> *hallowed be Thy name;*
> *Thy kingdom come;*
> *Thy will be done;*
> *on earth as it is in heaven.*[62]

---

62. Northumbria Community, *Celtic Daily Prayer*, 20.

3

Sustained by the Faith Community

Introduction

BONHOEFFER'S FAITH RESTED IN and was shaped by his relationship with the crucified and risen Christ. In the person and work of Christ, Bonhoeffer saw God's gracious way for the renewal of humanity and the restoration of all things, for he believed that the Lordship of Christ not only shaped individual lives and the church community, but also the entire social order. Thus in Christ, Bonhoeffer saw hope for the whole world.

Because Bonhoeffer was deeply concerned about the way society was becoming deformed through Nazi ideology, he called the church to be more fully committed to Christ and to live as a prophetic community that would challenge the political idolatry of his time. The heart of his strategy was not simply to call the church to be more socially active, but rather to call the faith community to become more truly *"Christus praesens"*[1] by living in conformity to Christ and his way of being in the world. He felt the church was called to live as a witness to Christ and a reflection of the redemptive impact that Christ could have in the world.

Because Bonhoeffer's Christology is so intimately linked with his ecclesiology, his writing focuses not only on what the church should *do*, but also what the church should *be*.

---

1. Bonhoeffer, *Works,* vol. 12, *Berlin 1932–1933,* 83.

This reflects a pastoral spirituality that is particularly relevant for our day, as the church in the West seems to be under attack from secular culture, and many Christians have become disaffected and disconnected from the church. At the same time, the church in the Majority World is facing dire poverty, unjust political institutions, flamboyant charismatic leaders, and is often characterized by an acquiescent laity.

In exploring what Bonhoeffer has to say about the church, we will revisit the familiar themes of the word, the sacramental life of the church, worship as a way of life, the church as a fellowship community, and the church as a suffering servant.

Though Bonhoeffer accepts the necessary ecclesiastical structures of the church, those structures do not constitute the heart of the church, for "the most precious thing in Christianity is Jesus Christ Himself."[2] Moreover, Christ is not only "the center and strength of the Bible, of the church, and of theology, but also of humanity, of reason, of justice, and of culture."[3]

Because Bonhoeffer does not have a narrow or limited view of Christ and his ministry, he does not have a narrow view of the task and mission of the church. He writes that the church's full acknowledgment and commitment to Christ plunges Christians into "the wide range of [God's] dominion."[4]

But this does not mean that the church should seek social and political power for itself, for the purpose of the church is not to orchestrate a superior Christian culture. Rather, the church is called to proclaim and *live* the crucified Christ, "who found no shelter in the world," but who is our true home, in whom we "seek sanctuary."[5]

In following Christ, the church seeks to be a healing and restorative presence in the world and to call others to embrace Christ. Just as Christ rejected spurious power when he was tempted in the desert, the church must do the same. Because the church in its mission "neither renders the human reality independent nor destroys it,"[6] the church is both *affirming* of society and culture while also *rejecting* its idolatrous pretensions and distortions. The faith community calls into question all forms of human arrogance and self-sufficiency that distort the goodness of life that God wills for all.

2. Bonhoeffer, *Ethics*, 58.
3. Bonhoeffer, *Ethics*, 58.
4. Bonhoeffer, *Ethics*, 60.
5. Bonhoeffer, *Ethics*, 61.
6. Bonhoeffer, *Ethics*, 131.

Sustained by the Faith Community

For Bonhoeffer, the church is a sustained community of grace that is brought into God's love through the salvific work of Christ and the enabling Spirit. *Christ is present* to the church as Word, sacrament, and fellowship, and the church *expresses Christ* through its worship, prayer, and service.

3:1

The Living Word

The grass withers, the flower fades,
when the breath of the Lord blows upon it;
. . . but the word of our God will stand forever.

—Isaiah 40:7–8

Bonhoeffer takes Scripture seriously, as he sees it as the proclamation of the Living Word, Jesus Christ. He describes the power of the "Bible and . . . the proclamation of [the] gospel" as having "its own beauty," and he writes that our finest response to its winsome call is to have "an obedient heart."[7]

Expounding on this important theme, he writes that "the living Christ" is the key to discipleship, for *"only [the one] who believes is obedient and only [the one] who is obedient believes."*[8]

Early in Bonhoeffer's life, he moved away from a "more academic" orientation to Scripture and towards a costly discipleship in obedience to Christ.[9] After experiencing an "inner clarity and honesty," he started "to take the Sermon on the Mount seriously."[10] Later, he wrote *The Cost of Discipleship* as a sustained reflection on the Sermon of the Mount, with a particular focus on the Beatitudes. For Bonhoeffer, the heart of a costly discipleship is to live in reliance "solely on Christ" as part of a "visible" community of faith.[11]

Bonhoeffer's focus on the Gospels did not mean that he was not interested in the rest of Scripture, but he felt that a lot of theological scholarship

---

7. Bonhoeffer, *Works*, vol. 13, *London 1933–1935*, 355.
8. Bonhoeffer, *Cost of Discipleship*, 50, 54 (emphasis in original).
9. Bonhoeffer, *Works*, vol. 13, *London 1933–1935*, 284.
10. Bonhoeffer, *Works*, vol. 13, 285.
11. Bonhoeffer, *Cost of Discipleship*, 101, 139.

Sustained by the Faith Community

could only bear limited fruit, whereas "the Scriptures deliver to us" Christ himself because "the risen one encounters us" in the Bible.[12]

Bonhoeffer speaks of "Christ as Word," which he describes as Christ in "the spoken Word of preaching."[13] In the church's proclamation, he explains that "a mystery takes place, a miracle," which is that "the grace of God . . . speaks to us, knocks on our door, asks questions, warns us, . . . alarms us, . . . and makes us joyful again and free and sure."[14] He is adamant that the word of preaching is not merely a pious message of comfort, but a word of "judgement and forgiveness."[15] In this double message, he says that "God's Word in Jesus Christ pronounces [us] guilty" and also "pronounces [us] free and righteous."[16]

For Bonhoeffer, God the Son reveals the face of God the Father, and "because faith sees God in Christ, it sees God."[17] Bonhoeffer celebrates the mystery that Christ "is the center of human existence, of history, and of nature."[18] Moreover, he rejoices that through Christ, "God will establish God's kingdom and rule."[19] By looking to the cross of Christ, our eyes will be opened so that we can see that "God will make everything new again," for despite life's difficulties, "God will cause grace and compassion to radiate over the dark guilt of our century and the human race."[20]

The full scope of God's redemptive work is centered in Christ, and those who join with Christ are called to participate in *all* that God seeks to do in renewing *all* things. But to take up this challenge, Bonhoeffer calls us to "risk placing our lives on Jesus' word."[21]

> *Jesus, you are the shepherd of us all.*
> *I pray that those who need you in this moment would not be found lacking.*
> *You lead them to calm waters, infusing them with new strength.*
> *You guide them on the path of justice for the sake of your name.*[22]

---

12. Bonhoeffer, *Christ the Center*, 73-74.
13. *Christ the Center*, 49, 51.
14. Bonhoeffer, *Works*, vol. 13, *London 1933-1935*, 323.
15. Bonhoeffer, *Christ the Center*, 52.
16. Bonhoeffer, *Works*, vol. 5, *Life Together/Prayer Book of the Bible*, 31.
17. Bonhoeffer, *Works*, vol. 10, *Barcelona, Berlin, New York 1928-1931*, 466.
18. Bonhoeffer, *Christ the Center*, 60.
19. Bonhoeffer, *Works*, vol. 9, *Young Bonhoeffer, 1918-1927*, 559.
20. Bonhoeffer, *Works*, vol. 10, *Barcelona, Berlin, New York 1928-1931*, 358-359.
21. Bonhoeffer, *Works*, vol. 9, *Young Bonhoeffer, 1918-1927*, 560.
22. Carvalhaes, *Liturgies from Below*, 154.

3:2

The Sacramental Life: Baptism

Therefore, we have been buried with him by baptism into his death, so that, just as Christ was raised from the dead by the glory of the Father, so, we too might walk in newness of life.

—ROMANS 6:4

Throughout Bonhoeffer's writings, he describes baptism as a sacramental rite that reflects several multidirectional realities of faith.

Through baptism, we are incorporated *into* Christ and become *identified with* Christ and his purposes for the world. As Bonhoeffer puts it, baptism reflects a "washing away of sin, being born again, dying and rising with Christ, conformation with the image of Christ."[23]

Thus baptism is not a mere ritual of the institutional church, but a deeply transformative event. Bonhoeffer stresses that baptism "betokens a *breach*," explaining that "in baptism [one] becomes Christ's own possession."[24] Therefore one no longer belongs to the world, but "belongs to Christ alone."[25] This does not mean that we withdraw from the world, but rather that our "relationship with the world is mediated through [Jesus Christ]."[26] Through faith in Jesus Christ, we seek to love and engage the whole world.

In this way, Bonhoeffer sees baptism as a continuance. Rather than freezing its significance into a past event, he describes how the "baptized live . . . by a constant renewal of . . . faith in the death of Christ."[27]

---

23. Bonhoeffer, *Works*, vol. 16, *Conspiracy and Imprisonment 1940–1945*, 556–57.
24. Bonhoeffer, *Cost of Discipleship*, 206.
25. Bonhoeffer, *Cost of Discipleship*, 207.
26. Bonhoeffer, *Cost of Discipleship*, 207.
27. Bonhoeffer, *Cost of Discipleship*, 210.

Bonhoeffer describes another dimension of baptism, which is that when we join "the fellowship of the baptized," we become "grafted on to the visible body of Christ."[28] As we participate in the life of the church community, we live out a "baptismal death," which will involve "suffering 'for him' [Christ]" as a "vicarious activity" in relation to the world.[29]

Bonhoeffer also stresses the "connection of baptism and the gift of the Spirit."[30] He describes the baptized as "the house where the Holy Spirit has made his dwelling."[31] Thus "the fellowship of the baptized" is the fellowship of the Spirit. He explains that the Holy Spirit creates "the moment of unity" of the faith community and empowers it in its witness and service to the world.[32] Moreover, he writes that all "holy work . . . lies with the Holy Spirit."[33]

Bonhoeffer is clear that the sacrament of baptism in the church should issue forth in a sacramental *way of life* in the community. Thus our "baptismal death" is not restricted to the inner life of the church, but becomes "the fountain of grace" through which we live a life of suffering service in the world.[34]

> *Jesus commanded his disciples to baptize people*
> *in God's holy name,*
> *so that the message of love and recreation*
> *would bless the whole world.*
> *In baptism, we are invited*
> *to begin and renew a journey*
> *that calls us to show God's love in words and actions*
> *that uplift community.*[35]

---

28. Bonhoeffer, *Cost of Discipleship*, 219, 209.
29. Bonhoeffer, *Cost of Discipleship*, 207, 220.
30. Bonhoeffer, *Works*, vol. 9, *Young Bonhoeffer, 1918–1927*, 446.
31. Bonhoeffer, *Cost of Discipleship*, 210.
32. Bonhoeffer, *Works*, vol. 9, *Young Bonhoeffer, 1918–1927*, 446.
33. Bonhoeffer, *Works*, vol. 9, 334.
34. Bonhoeffer, *Cost of Discipleship*, 207.
35. Carvalhaes, *Liturgies from Below*, 114.

3:3

The Sacramental Life: Holy Communion

Then he took a loaf of bread, and when he had given thanks, he broke it and gave it to them, saying, "This is my body, which is given for you. Do this is remembrance of me." And he did the same with the cup after supper, saying, "This cup that is poured out for you is the new covenant in my blood."
—Luke 22:19–21

Bonhoeffer sees a profound connection between Christ and the faith community, noting that Christ is both "present *as* Church" and "*in* the Church."[36] He stresses the connection between the sacraments and the nature of what it means to be church, describing the church as a "baptismal and eucharistic congregation."[37] He also emphasizes that the common sacramental life of the church gives testimony to the "concrete humanity of the Son of God."[38]

In the sacrament of the Eucharist, the community of faith receives the gift of the life-giving presence of Christ, through the Spirit, as our food and drink for the journey of faith, service, and suffering. Moreover, as Bonhoeffer puts it, "when this Word comes, the Holy Spirit comes, showing to Christians, both individually and corporately, the gifts of the incarnate Christ."[39] Thus in the life of the faith community, Christ is Word, sacrament, and community.[40]

Bonhoeffer emphasizes that the Lord's Supper is a gift to each person in the faith community and also a gift to the community as a whole, for in

---

36. Bonhoeffer, *Christ the Center*, 58 (emphasis in original).
37. Bonhoeffer, *Cost of Discipleship*, 226.
38. Bonhoeffer, *Cost of Discipleship*, 229.
39. Bonhoeffer, *Cost of Discipleship*, 225.
40. Bonhoeffer, *Christ the Center*, 49–59.

the church, "*Christ gives community with himself.*"⁴¹ In Christ, we are bound together and sustained together in a common life.

In further elaborating on the Eucharist, Bonhoeffer describes this sacramental feast as a gathering of "all those who are serious about submitting their will to God's rule in the Realm of Christ."⁴² As such, Holy Communion is a reflection of an "obedient symbolism."⁴³

Bonhoeffer makes several other important observations regarding the nature of Holy Communion.

First, he reminds us of the mystery of humiliation. Christ *stoops down* to engage us by coming to us through the lowly elements of bread and wine. Christ exists "as sacrament in the church . . . *because* he is the Humiliated One."⁴⁴

Second, in the sacrament of communion, Christ *draws close* to us. As Bonhoeffer describes it, "He is by our side as a creature, in our midst as a brother among brothers and sisters."⁴⁵

Third, the Eucharist is our food and drink in Christ, and this "fosters and sustains our fellowship."⁴⁶

Finally, the church gains visibility through its sacramental life, and its fellowship in Christ is marked by its need to remain in Christ. Bonhoeffer explains that in Acts 2 and 4, the "infant church was a visible community which all the world could see."⁴⁷

As followers of Christ, it is important to remember that we don't engage the sacramental life as those who are receiving special privileges, but as *confessing sinners*. As forgiven ones, we find an "inexpressible joy in his presence" in the communion meal.⁴⁸

> *As we lift this bread, asking you to consecrate it,*
> *bless our land to flow with milk and honey . . .*
> *As we break it, break the hearts of the empire and the chains of the oppressed.*
> *As it is shared among us,*
> *may we embrace each other's burdens in solidarity and love.*

---

41. Bonhoeffer, *Works*, vol. 1, *Sanctorum Communio*, 243 (emphasis in original).
42. Bonhoeffer, *Works*, vol. 1, 242.
43. Bonhoeffer, *Works*, vol. 1, 244.
44. Bonhoeffer, *Works*, vol. 12, *Berlin 1932–1933*, 322 (emphasis in original).
45. Bonhoeffer, *Works*, vol. 12, 322.
46. Bonhoeffer, *Cost of Discipleship*, 215.
47. Bonhoeffer, *Cost of Discipleship*, 229.
48. Bonhoeffer, *Works*, vol. 12, *Berlin 1932–1933*, 470.

In the Shadow of a Rugged Cross

As we lift this cup,
we remember that our people are crushed but they are not destroyed . . .
as we share it, may we be reminded that we share the same blood,
we are a family of hope.[49]

---

49. Carvalhaes, *Liturgies from Below*, 133.

3:4

Worship: A Way of Life

O come, let us worship and bow down,
let us kneel before the Lord, our Maker!

—Psalm 95:6

It is possible to cast Bonhoeffer as a political activist, but this does not do full justice to his life and work, for Bonhoeffer also lived a life of faith that was oriented to loving God, faithfully following Christ, living in the power of the Spirit, serving the church and the world, and bearing prophetic witness in response to the injustices of his day.

For Bonhoeffer, all of these dimensions of his life of faith formed a seamless garment, both personally and communally.

Bonhoeffer writes that "holy work . . . lies with the Spirit," and such "holy work" includes all the dimensions of life, including the life of worship.[50] Bonhoeffer notes how the Spirit brings the Word that offers "the grace of God . . . and makes us joyful again and free and sure."[51] In this way, worship— our orientation towards God in praise and gratitude—is the fruit of God's action in our lives.

To probe more deeply into the nature of worship, Bonhoeffer uses an analogy to explain that "the human soul is a harp, and the word of God, as it touches the soul, is the harpist."[52] Whenever we are touched by the Word and the Spirit, worship wells up and spills out to the glory of God. Bonhoeffer celebrates this movement of the Spirit, writing that "out of these obedient hearts grew the visible work and audible song to the glory of God and Jesus Christ."[53]

---

50. Bonhoeffer, *Works*, vol. 9, *Young Bonhoeffer, 1918–1927*, 334.
51. Bonhoeffer, *Works*, vol. 13, *London 1933–1935*, 323.
52. Bonhoeffer, *Works*, vol. 13, 355.
53. Bonhoeffer, *Works*, vol, 13, 355.

Even though Bonhoeffer emphasizes that the heart of worship occurs when our "gaze is not upon our own needs but on God's majesty and glory,"[54] he nevertheless celebrates that worship can raise "up those who are cast down" and can bring "sinners to repentance in the face of God's goodness."[55] He continues that singing unto the Lord can make "the sinner to turn around, the homeless to come home, the stubborn weep, and those who weep rejoice."[56] Thus he believes that worship through song is a God-honoring dimension in the Christian's life that also brings joy and healing.

In wrestling with the Nazification of the Lutheran church, Bonhoeffer was particularly concerned about two aspects of worship in the church.

First, he raised the most basic question: *whom do we worship?* Bonhoeffer's concern was that humanity has a tendency "to worship its own accomplishments."[57] Thus idolatry is an ever-present specter that needs to be resisted. In all our worship, God must be given the only rightful place.

Second, Bonhoeffer was concerned that Hitler was viewed by many as a sort of messiah, and so people in the church were worshipping Hitler and his ideology rather than God. He felt that individuals in the church were surrendering "ultimate responsibility" to Hitler as the leader,[58] but for the Christian, "it is to God that the individual is responsible."[59] Thus he emphasized that in the Confessing Church, the "worship of God and not of humankind . . . takes place at the altar."[60]

Third, Bonhoeffer was adamant that no one should be excluded from the worship of God due to race or ethnicity. He rejected the political Aryan paragraph, with its "exclusion of . . . Jewish Christians from the communion of worship."[61] He emphasized that if *any* are excluded from communion, then *all* are excluded, because the community of faith is one body in Christ.

Bonhoeffer makes it clear that all Christian worship should be God-oriented, church-celebrated, and prophetic in its critique of anyone who undermines the welcome of God in Christ.

---

54. Bonhoeffer, *Works*, vol. 15, *Theological Education Underground 1937–1940*, 328.
55. Bonhoeffer, *Works*, vol, 13, *London 1933–1935*, 357.
56. Bonhoeffer, *Works*, vol. 13, 357.
57. Bonhoeffer, *Works*, vol. 12, *Berlin 1932–1933*, 475.
58. Bonhoeffer, *Works*, vol. 12, 277.
59. Bonhoeffer, *Works*, vol. 12, 281.
60. Bonhoeffer, *Works*, vol. 12, 462–63.
61. Bonhoeffer, *Works*, vol. 12, 373.

Sustained by the Faith Community

Thus, my mind,
filled with the fruits
of its own reflection upon the teaching of Scripture,
rested with assurance,
as on some peaceful watchtower . . .
in the conviction that [God's] greatness
is too vast for our comprehension,
but not for our faith.[62]

---

62. From Hilary of Poitiers (c. 300–367). Quoted in Ringma and Alexander, eds., *Of Martyrs, Monks, and Mystics,* 391.

3:5

Life Together

All who believed were together and had all things in common; they would sell their possessions and goods and distribute the proceeds to all, as any had need.

—Acts 2:44–45

Bonhoeffer's writing celebrates Christ's presence in and lordship over all, insisting that Christ "exists" "in Word, Sacrament, and Church" and also "in the center of human existence, of history and of nature."[63] Moreover, he stresses that Christ "is the center and strength of the Bible, of the Church, and of theology, but also of humanity, of reason, of justice, and of culture."[64]

Bonhoeffer argues that "the church is the real body of Christ on earth," serving as the "space of proclamation, the space of order, the space of the Christian life."[65] But he also writes that a Christian community is fundamentally the same as the body of Christ, for it is also "held together solely in Christ."[66]

Thus for Bonhoeffer, one's participation in the church and one's service in Christian community are complementary forms of life together. From his experience of training the clergy of the Confessing Church in the setting of communal living, he wrote *Life Together*, which has become a classic on Christian community.

Because the parish church and any form of intentional Christian community are formed and shaped *in* Christ, they are an embodiment *of* Christ—not merely a "wish dream."[67] Moreover, Christians can only live

---

63. Bonhoeffer, *Christ the Center*, 59–60.
64. Bonhoeffer, *Ethics*, 58.
65. Bonhoeffer, *Works*, vol. 15, *Theological Education Underground 1937–1940*, 422.
66. Bonhoeffer, *Life Together*, 18.
67. Bonhoeffer, *Life Together*, 26.

"community through... and in Jesus Christ," solely by "God's justification."[68] Thus he writes that a communal form of life together is a "sign of the gracious presence of the triune God," and the fellowship of such a community is "a gift of grace."[69] A Christian community can give more specific expression to this "gift of grace" by sharing living space, meals, common work, spiritual practices, and common forms of witness and service.

Yet a shared life does not involve a loss of personal identity, for life in community is both a life alone and a life together. When we share life together, we recognize how much we need Christ and how much we need our fellow travelers in the faith, but we don't lose our identity, agency, and our personal responsibility.

Moreover, Bonhoeffer emphasizes that while we are bound together in Christ, "Christ [also] stands between the lover and the others he loves."[70] As Bonhoeffer puts it so eloquently, "When God was merciful to us, we learned to be merciful with our brethren.... What God did to us, we then owed to others."[71]

In our time, we need to recover Bonhoeffer's challenge to see both the church and Christian community as an embodiment of Christ in the world so that we might live as a "sign of the gracious presence of the triune God" and be "a gift of grace" to those around us.[72]

Enable us to touch our neighbors and build solidarities.
Enable us to build peace
and institute justice in our relationships.
Enable us to break the barriers
that are destroying our communities.
Enable us to bridge the gaps that separate us from each other.[73]

---

68. Bonhoeffer, *Life Together*, 21, 22.
69. Bonhoeffer, *Life Together*, 20.
70. Bonhoeffer, *Life Together*, 35.
71. Bonhoeffer, *Life Together*, 24–25.
72. Bonhoeffer, *Life Together*, 20.
73. Carvalhaes, *Liturgies from Below*, 272.

3:6

Witness and Service

"Thus it is written, that the Messiah is to suffer and to rise from the dead on the third day, and that repentance and forgiveness of sins is to be proclaimed in his name to all nations . . . You are witnesses of these things. And see, I am sending upon you what my Father promised; so stay here in the city until you have been clothed with power from on high."

—Luke 24:46–49

As a pastor, theologian, and activist, Bonhoeffer sought the renewal of the church and the reshaping of society by calling Christians to embody a Christ-formed life amidst the Nazification of the church and nation and the difficult realities of World War II.

Rather than being stunned into hopelessness and resignation in light of these troubling circumstances, he was sustained by Christ, who called him to new life through the resurrection power of the Spirit and also to suffer for the sake of Christ. Empowered by the Holy Spirit, Bonhoeffer lived a life of costly discipleship, witness, and service, in concert with other Christ followers, on behalf of the church.

But Bonhoeffer was no solo hero, for he understood that his witness and service were rooted in Christ's salvific work for the restoration and renewal of all things. He writes that through the power of the cross and resurrection, "God will make everything new again."[74] Yet he emphasizes that restoration can only come through God alone, the "one before whom the mightiest powers crumble."[75]

---

74. Bonhoeffer, *Works*, vol. 10, *Barcelona, Berlin, New York 1928–1931*, 358.
75. Bonhoeffer, *Works*, vol. 16, *Conspiracy and Imprisonment 1940–1945*, 625.

Moreover, Bonhoeffer insists that change can only come through "God's revelation in Christ," which is "God's word to the present."[76] He also makes it clear that we must rely on the Spirit, who "effectively" brings this revelation "to the heart of the hearers."[77] And he defines the church as a "community of sinners,"[78] arguing that the faith community is "a church that is always penitent."[79]

At the same time, Bonhoeffer proclaims that living a life of witness and service has profound implications, for a life of faith is "only *true* in discipleship" and must involve love of neighbor, which is "a *parable* for our love of God."[80] This life of faith calls us to "sacrifice, prayer, and forgiveness" and also binds us "to the earth, to misery, to hunger, to death," bringing us into the "most profound solidarity with the world."[81]

He identifies the two essential tasks of the church as bringing the hope of the gospel to the world and calling into question all that distorts God's goodness in the world. To fulfill these important commissions, Bonhoeffer calls the faith community to engage culture, society, and the state.

Bonhoeffer describes this vocation of the church as the "breaching of the world and its laws."[82] In other words, we are not only to *question* what is unjust in our world, but to *undo* the wrong in our world. He points out that this is only possible when the faith community lives as a servant of the "kingdom of the resurrection," which *"is miraculous."*[83]

Thus Bonhoeffer insists that the church should question the state, provide services "to the victims of the state's actions," and "not just . . . bind up the wounds of the victims beneath the wheel, but . . . seize the wheel itself."[84]

> *We pray that under the power of the spirit of justice and love,*
> *we may resist every evil perpetuated by empire.*
> *We pray that we may speak for justice*
> *and give voice to the voiceless . . .*

---

76. Bonhoeffer, *Works*, vol. 10, *Barcelona, Berlin, New York 1928–1931*, 382.
77. Bonhoeffer, *Works*, vol. 1, *Sanctorum Communio*, 158.
78. Bonhoeffer, *Works*, vol. 12, *Berlin 1932–1933*, 403.
79. Bonhoeffer, *Works*, vol. 12, 284.
80. Bonhoeffer, *Works*, vol. 12, 259, 261 (emphasis in original).
81. Bonhoeffer, *Works*, vol. 12, 263, 289.
82. Bonhoeffer, *Works*, vol. 12, 264.
83. Bonhoeffer, *Works*, vol. 12, 291.
84. Bonhoeffer, *Works*, vol. 12, 365.

In the Shadow of a Rugged Cross

We pray that together we may receive the fullness of life promised by our Lord Jesus Christ.[85]

---

85. Carvalhaes, *Liturgies from Below*, 206.

4

Sustained by the Spirit

Introduction

EVERYWHERE BONHOEFFER LOOKED, HE faced challenges: within his country and the compromised church of the state, amidst the radical changes brought about by fascism and the scourge of World War II, and in the lack of courage and resolve in the Confessing Church.

Wherever Bonhoeffer turned and tried to focus his energies in creative resistance, he encountered difficulties and failure: the closure of his illegal seminary, the inability of church leaders in the UK to hear his pleas for help, the Abwehr's unsuccessful attempts to eradicate Hitler.

But Bonhoeffer did not give up. He was not defeated—not even during his years in prison as he awaited the possibility of death.

There is far more at play here than stoicism, a strong personality, or the blessings of family. For in all of these circumstances, Bonhoeffer was sustained by his Christian faith and his dynamic relationship with Christ.

Nourished by spiritual practices, he sought to live the Sermon on the Mount in the context of shared community life while enunciating a prophetic voice that called the social and political powers of his day to hear Christ's challenge of justice and peacemaking, conversion and restoration.

Central to Bonhoeffer's faith was his conviction that Christ was Lord over *all* of life, and therefore he believed he was called to obey both the written word and the Living Word, Jesus Christ. This way of life was continually animated by Bonhoeffer's openness to the sustaining presence of the Holy Spirit.

Bonhoeffer has been aptly described as a christological theologian, for he proclaimed and lived a christological spirituality. But he was also a man of the Spirit—a theme that is often underplayed in studies of his life and work. In this section, we will gain a sense of the richness of Bonhoeffer's pneumatology.

Throughout Bonhoeffer's writings, he maintains a dynamic link between the Word and the Spirit. He writes that "when the Holy Scriptures are brought to life in a church, the Holy Spirit comes down from the eternal throne, into our hearts."[1] Thus the Spirit makes the Word of God active, penetrating, and life-changing.

Moreover, the Spirit draws us to an obedient listening of the word, for "the Holy Spirit . . . would command loyal service to the gospel."[2] In other words, the follower of Jesus who has received the gift of the Spirit is drawn by the Spirit to listen faithfully to Scripture for personal transformation and social engagement. Thus Bonhoeffer is not only committed to a pneumatological interpretation of Scripture,[3] but believes in the pneumatological enhancement and empowerment of the whole of a Christian's life.

Following are some broad themes to keep in mind as we explore Bonhoeffer's engagement with the Holy Spirit in this section.

First, in following Jesus, we are not simply called to believe the good news of the gospel about Christ's salvific death and resurrection, for the gospel must also form and animate our lives. This is the happy task of the Spirit.

Second, when we engage Scripture, our reading should not only remain at the intellectual level, for the word is always seeking to make a revelatory impact. Again, this is the work of the Spirit.

Third, when we become part of a faith community, we are not simply joining a religious institution, but the mystical body of Christ. Yet we can only experience this mystery through the life-giving Spirit, who creates community.

Fourth, in living the Christian life and engaging the spiritual disciplines, we are not simply called to persevere through all seasons, for Christ gives us the gift of the Holy Spirit to sustain us in our life of prayer and contemplation.

1. Bonhoeffer, *Works,* vol. 13, *London 1933–1935,* 323.
2. Bonhoeffer, *Works,* vol. 9, *Young Bonhoeffer, 1918–1927,* 268.
3. Bonhoeffer, *Works,* vol. 9, 285–300.

Fifth, in our work of witness and service, we need to rely on more than our own abilities, for if our service is to be fruitful, we need the Spirit to guide and empower us.

Finally, Bonhoeffer challenges us that in times of great trial and difficulty, we need more than patient endurance, for we can trust that "the entire fullness of the Holy Spirit wants to enfold and ripen" in us.[4]

---

4. Bonhoeffer, *Works*, vol. 16, *Conspiracy and Imprisonment 1940–1945*, 628.

4:1

Bound to Christ

"When the Spirit of truth comes, he will guide you into all the truth; for he will not speak on his own, but will speak whatever he hears . . . He will glorify me, because he will take what is mine and declare it to you."

—JOHN 16:13–14

Bonhoeffer's spirituality can help us overcome the common and unhealthy dichotomy between Word and Spirit. Rather than focusing on the Word and neglecting the Spirit, on the one hand, or giving free rein to a freewheeling Spirit that ignores the Word (and often ends up in mystical vagaries), on the other, Bonhoeffer holds Word and Spirit together.

He also emphasizes the dynamic relationship between Jesus Christ, the Living Word, and the Holy Spirit. He explains that "God himself came in Jesus Christ" and that Christ "breaks as the holy Ghost into the circle of [humankind]."[5] Later, he writes that God, "who in Jesus Christ" has loved us "even unto death," also "in the Holy Spirit opens our hearts."[6] Put simply, the Spirit is Christ's gift, who brings Christ home to dwell within us, sustain us, and empower us.

Bonhoeffer recognizes the wide scope of the Holy Spirit's operations, generalizing that "the Holy Spirit shows us the *way of the truth to the light.*"[7] But he also highlights a narrower focus, asserting that "the *only* ministry of the Holy Spirit consists *in the witness to Jesus Christ.*"[8] In this section, I will reflect further on this claim, particularly its implications for Christian spirituality.

---

5. Bonhoeffer, *Works*, vol. 10, *Barcelona, Berlin, New York 1928–1931*, 473.

6. Bonhoeffer, *Works*, vol. 13, *London 1933–1935*, 363.

7. Bonhoeffer, *Works*, vol. 15, *Theological Education Underground 1937–1940*, 562 (emphasis in original).

8. Bonhoeffer, *Works*, vol. 15, 557 (emphasis in original).

Sustained by the Spirit

Spirituality can mean almost anything in our present-day world—a realm of inwardness, reflection, and meditation, or an experience of transcendence, creativity, enlightenment, and imagination. This has much to do with twenty-first-century attempts to know beyond the more dominant scientistic and rationalistic ways of understanding.

While this may augur well for richer ways of understanding ourselves and the human condition, it does not bring us to the heart of Christian spirituality, which has to do with faith in Jesus Christ and our ongoing relationship with Christ through the Spirit. For Christians, this relationship should animate who we are and all that we seek to do. Thus Bonhoeffer is concerned with bringing the presence of Jesus Christ and the work of the Holy Spirit into a direct and dynamic relationship.

The nature of this relationship is important, for the Holy Spirit makes the gospel *alive* so that it can speak with power to bring us to Christ. Because our birthing into Christ happens through the Holy Spirit, the Spirit is a gift of grace, given by God's unlimited generosity. As Bonhoeffer puts it, "Christ can only be grasped in the Spirit."[9]

Having grasped Christ in the Spirit, Christ grows and takes fuller shape in us through both the Spirit and the Word. As the Spirit "weaves" faith in Christ into the very fabric of our lives, "the Holy Spirit creates a new person."[10] As new creations, we are indwelt by Christ.

With Christ "growing" in us, the Spirit seeks to bring forth the life of Christ through us into the world. Empowered by the Spirit, the presence of Christ also unfolds into the world through the faith community.

Moreover, through the Spirit, the follower of Christ "can do, what he [she] wants to do."[11] In other words, the believer is empowered by the Spirit to enact the good news of Christ to the degree that his/her "deeds are also sanctified."[12]

This displays the wonderful synchronicity that is at play in the work of the Spirit, which births and unfolds Christ into the world through his followers so that the world might know that Christ is "the way, and the truth, and the life" (John 14:6).

Thus, he declared the work of the Spirit.
This, then, is the Paraclete's guiding office:

9. Bonhoeffer, *Works*, vol. 9, *Young Bonhoeffer, 1918–1927*, 340.
10. Bonhoeffer, *Works*, vol. 9, 341.
11. *Works*, vol. 10, *Barcelona, Berlin, New York 1928–1931*, 448.
12. Bonhoeffer, *Works*, vol. 10, 448.

the direction of discipline,
the revelation of the Scriptures,
the reformation of the intellect,
the advancement towards the "better things."[13]

---

13. From Tertullian (c. 160–220). Quoted in Ringma and Alexander, eds., *Of Martyrs, Monks, and Mystics*, 155.

4:2

Comfort in Times of Difficulty

Create in me a clean heart, O God,
and put a new and right spirit within me.
Do not cast me away from your presence,
and do not take your holy spirit from me.
Restore to me the joy of your salvation,
and sustain in me a willing spirit.

—Psalm 51:10–12

So much of the presence of the Spirit in our lives is well beyond our awareness, and the work of the Spirit in sustaining us often happens without our perceiving it. Sadly, the Spirit can be a taken-for-granted participant in our lives—and neglecting the Spirit may well be our greatest folly.

Many in the West live under the illusion that we are self-made and self-determined creatures. We tend to have little sense of the inter-relationality of life and little awareness that we need spiritual nourishment in order to live well. In Bonhoeffer's day, he lamented how "the teaching about the Holy Spirit has largely faded and been forgotten."[14] At times, as during periods of renewal, we live with a greater awareness of the Spirit, but this often fades because we so easily begin to try to plan, manipulate, and manage the Spirit's work.

Bonhoeffer offers an important corrective, for he teaches us about the presence of the Spirit during times of difficulty and trial. Rather than taking these times for granted, reacting to them, or denying them, Bonhoeffer encourages us to become more fully *aware* and *responsive* to the Holy Spirit. During times of difficulty, he suggests that the Holy Spirit, as the Paraclete,

---

14. Bonhoeffer, *Works*, vol. 15, *Theological Education Underground 1937–1940*, 557.

comes alongside of us, and so we need to make "full space within us" for the Spirit's presence.[15]

Since Bonhoeffer certainly lived in the midst of great difficulty, it is important to heed his voice. During times of trial, he instructs us not to give in to passive resignation, but to be alert and expectant because "the entire fullness of the Holy Spirit wants to unfold and ripen" in us.[16] There are many reasons that the Spirit might become more active during times of trial.

First, when we face difficulties, we are much more aware of our need for help and therefore more open to the Spirit's assistance. Thus we may become more prayerful and receptive to God's action in our lives.

Second, it is in the Spirit's nature to come alongside us in order to help and assist us. Our vulnerability galvanizes the Spirit into action.

Third, when we are needy and vulnerable, the Spirit can grow in us. Hence Bonhoeffer says that the Spirit can take up "full space within us."[17] In other words, the Spirit seeks to take *fuller possession* of us—not in order to control us, but to nurture, sustain, and empower us.

Finally, Bonhoeffer highlights that the work of the Spirit in our lives is "for the sake of God, for the sake of others, and for our own sake."[18] The Spirit is always seeking to draw us into greater intimacy with the Father, the Son, and all who are in need. As we grow in intimacy with the Father and the Son, we are enriched—and out of this enrichment, we are able to bless others.

> *God sees you and calls you by name.*
> *He calls you to stand firm in the face of oppression and injustice.*
> *May you stand firm then*
> *as the Holy Spirit enlivens your hope,*
> *as Jesus Christ renews your faith,*
> *as God enfolds you in love.*[19]

---

15. Bonhoeffer, *Works*, vol. 16, *Conspiracy and Imprisonment 1940–1945*, 628.
16. Bonhoeffer, *Works*, vol. 16, 628.
17. Bonhoeffer, *Works*, vol. 16, 628.
18. Bonhoeffer, *Works*, vol. 16, 628.
19. Carvalhaes, *Liturgies from Below*, 48.

4:3

Discernment

For as in one body we have many members, and not all the members have the same function, so we, who are many, are one body in Christ, and individually we are members one of another. We have gifts that differ according to the grace given to us: prophecy, in proportion to faith; ministry, in ministering; the teacher, in teaching; the exhorter, in exhortation; the giver, in generosity; the leader, in diligence; the compassionate, in cheerfulness.

—Romans 12:4–8

When we embrace the great gift of the Holy Spirit, we need to be discerning, for what is most precious can so easily be distorted. If the Spirit we are following is not binding us to the word and to the person and work of Christ, we can be led into the side-alleys of subjectivism. We can make all sorts of claims that the Spirit "told" us to say or do something when, in fact, we are overriding the ever-gentle Spirit or letting our own imaginations run rife.

Bonhoeffer emphasizes that the Holy Spirit always seeks to bring us to Christ, and as such "into loyal service of the gospel."[20] He notes that "Christ can only be grasped in the Spirit."[21] But he also acknowledges the Spirit's creative work, for he says that "only the Spirit of God . . . can reveal to a chosen person the mystery of the future in a way that compels prophecy to strengthen believers and to warn unbelievers."[22]

In this statement, Bonhoeffer is certainly not saying that the Spirit gives us the ability to predict the future—such as insight about which horse to back in the races, how to expose the inner life of another person, or how

---

20. Bonhoeffer, *Works*, vol. 9, *Young Bonhoeffer, 1918-1927*, 268.
21. Bonhoeffer, *Works*, vol, 9, 340.
22. Bonhoeffer, *Works*, vol. 16, *Conspiracy and Imprisonment 1940-1945*, 612.

to elevate someone in order to control others through charismatic gifting. Not at all!

Rather, Bonhoeffer is talking about the Spirit-inspired gifting of *insight* and *discernment,* particularly regarding dimensions of life where goodness and justice are being perverted. Through Spirit-inspired insight, Christ can move us to issue forth a call for repentance and renewal.

Very early in Hitler's rise to power, Bonhoeffer challenged Hitler's concept of leadership and suggested an alternative christological understanding regarding the proper use of power. And right at the beginning of Hitler's policy of discrimination against Jews, Bonhoeffer raised a voice of protest. In light of these actions, one can say that Bonhoeffer discerned the necessity of exemplifying a prophetic spirituality.

It is important to understand that in the Christian tradition, the work of the Spirit is not only about prayer, but also a strident and persistent prophecy. Because the prophetic word challenges what is usually accepted and disturbs what is typically taken for granted, any prophetic spirituality will need to be sustained over a long period of time.

If the Spirit is prompted to "reveal . . . the mystery of the future . . . that compels prophecy," as Bonhoeffer argues, then prophecy has a double focus: both "to *strengthen* believers" and also "to *warn* unbelievers."[23]

This double focus is important. First, prophecy is for the community of faith, and its purpose is to call the community to become more fully embedded in the purposes of God. Second, prophecy is for the wider community, and its purpose is to call those in power to realize their limitations and to become more just under God's providential purposes.

Thus the voice of the Holy Spirit, who animates our Christian spirituality, speaks to our souls and also to the world of politics.

Holy Spirit comfort us, move in our world.
Bring peace to those who have lost their humanity.
Bring peace to those who have lost their sense of belonging . . .
Holy Spirit . . . turn desolate deserts into an oasis of hope.
Turn impassable seas into waters of life.
Holy Spirit, heal us, restore our hearts.[24]

---

23. Bonhoeffer, *Works*, vol. 16, 612.
24. Carvalhaes, *Liturgies from Below*, 219.

4:4

Empowerment

"And see, I am sending upon you what my Father promised; so stay here in the city until you have been clothed with power from on high."

—LUKE 24:49

The promised Holy Spirit enlightens us, brings Christ home to us, works the fruits of the Spirit into our lives, showers us with enabling gifts, and empowers us for service. Bonhoeffer is particularly clear on the importance of the Spirit in our service, for he insists that "*only in the possession of the Holy Spirit can the work of Christ be done.*"[25] Moreover, he argues that "the *only* ministry of the Holy Spirit consists *in the witness to Jesus Christ.*"[26] Taken together, these two statements create a very interesting dynamic.

First, the Spirit is concerned with the revelation of Christ and the work of bringing Christ home to people. Once we become oriented towards Christ and seek to live our lives in the way of Christ, we need the Spirit in order to bear witness to Christ and to serve the members of the faith community and those in the wider community in his name.

Second, service that is empowered by the Spirit has a very specific motivation and outworking. Simply put, the core motivation is not to develop a "programme," but rather to form an "attachment" to Christ.[27] The specific outworking of this motivation is not "to impose the gospel by force," but rather to embrace a service that involves suffering as a "vicarious activity."[28]

---

25. Bonhoeffer, *Works*, vol. 15, *Theological Education Underground 1937–1940*, 544 (emphasis in original).
26. Bonhoeffer, *Works*, vol. 15, 557 (emphasis in original).
27. Bonhoeffer, *Cost of Discipleship*, 49.
28. Bonhoeffer, *Cost of Discipleship*, 165, 220.

This needs some careful unpacking. First, Christian service is not a program or project that we devise, but a *vision* that is birthed by the presence of Christ through the Spirit in our lives and in the faith community. For this vision to unfold in the world, we have to listen to the gospel and the Spirit's groaning, trusting that what we hear will enlighten our lives and the community. Thus Christian service is always both personal and corporate.

Second, Christian service is christological and Christocentric, for it is about birthing Christ in the world so that the redemption and healing that he accomplished in his suffering and resurrection can continue to unfold.

Even though Bonhoeffer stresses that Christ "is present *as* Church" and "*in* the church," the birthing of Christ into the world does not only happen within the church.[29] In Christ's sacrificial death, he took upon himself the sin, brokenness, and alienation of the whole world and provided the way for healing and renewal of all. Moreover, in his resurrection, Christ embraced his lordship over *all* things. Thus Christ cannot be restricted to the church, as this could lead to a spirituality of inwardness and a world-denying form of Christianity.

Instead, Bonhoeffer celebrates that Christ is also "the center of human existence, of history, and of nature."[30] In Christ's presence amongst humanity, he stands triumphant where we have failed and shares his victory with us.[31] In his role in history, Christ is the "destroyer" of all false "messianic promises," and he will fulfill the true messianic promise.[32] Finally, in Christ, "enslaved nature is redeemed in hope."[33]

In other words, the Spirit is seeking to bring the *whole* Christ to us—not only the Christ of inward piety. Moreover, the Spirit is seeking to motivate, move, and inspire us to see Christ born in the whole world—not only in the church, but in the very fabric of our society and the redemption of the natural world.

Thus through the ages, the people of faith have prayed, "*Veni Spiritus Sanctus.*"

> *You who shepherd the lost and comfort the afflicted.*
> *Guide our hands to touch the untouchable.*
> *Our ears to listen to the hopeless.*

---

29. Bonhoeffer, *Christ the Center*, 58 (emphasis in original).
30. Bonhoeffer, *Christ the Center*, 60.
31. Bonhoeffer, *Christ the Center*, 61.
32. Bonhoeffer, *Christ the Center*, 62.
33. Bonhoeffer, *Christ the Center*, 65.

Our eyes to see the misery of others.
Our hearts to feel the pain of prisoners.
Empower us to take risks to be channels of healing and mercy.[34]

---

34. Carvalhaes, *Liturgies from Below,* 102.

4:5

In-Spirited

Now there are variety of gifts, but the same Spirit; and there are varieties of services, but the same Lord; and there are varieties of activities, but the same God who activates all of them in everyone. To each is given the manifestation of the Spirit for the common good.

—1 CORINTHIANS 12:4–7

Throughout Bonhoeffer's writings, he celebrates the work of the Spirit in the church. He writes that "at Pentecost our church was founded by the Holy Spirit," and right into the present, the "Holy Spirit will sustain it."[35] In other words, through the Holy Spirit, the faith community—the body of Christ—continues to bring Christ into our present moment. By seeking to be like Christ, the faith community lives as a sign, servant, and sacrament of the reign and presence of God. In this way, Bonhoeffer sees the church as a *repetition* of Christ in the world.

Yet the Spirit, not the church, brings people to Christ, for the word of Christ is "effectively brought to the heart of the hearers by the Spirit."[36] Having been captivated by this winsome word and brought into a living relationship with Christ, all who "hear" are also brought into the faith community. As Bonhoeffer puts it, "the Holy Spirit is the will of God that gathers individuals together to be the church-community."[37] He presses this home by describing the church as "Christ *existing as* church-community."[38] Putting this even more clearly, he proclaims, "The church is the presence of Christ in the same way that Christ is the presence of God.[39]

---

35. Bonhoeffer, *Works*, vol. 16, *Conspiracy and Imprisonment 1940–1945*, 48.
36. Bonhoeffer, *Works*, vol. 1, *Sanctorum Communio*, 158.
37. Bonhoeffer, *Works*, vol. 1, 143.
38. Bonhoeffer, *Works*, vol. 1, 190 (emphasis in original).
39. Bonhoeffer, *Works*, vol. 1, 138.

Thus Bonhoeffer does not see the church primarily as an institutional reality, but as a Spirit-inspired, Spirit-sustained, and Spirit-empowered entity that is grounded in Christ, the living Word. He makes the point that "no one is in the church-community who has not already been moved by the Spirit,"[40] for "in faith the Holy Spirit creates a new person."[41]

Christians, therefore, are *in-spirited*. Inspired by the Holy Spirit, they are oriented to Christ and to one another so that they can become a community of Christ through the Spirit.

There is much that the Holy Spirit seeks to do in shaping and forming the church community. The work of the Spirit in enriching the church is beautiful and all-pervasive, but it is never for the church alone. Rather, this work is for the revelation of God in the world concerning the gift of God's Son in making all things new.

The Spirit accompanies the gospel and brings home the good news within all who hear it, challenging us and leading us to *ongoing* conversion. As Bonhoeffer notes, "contrition is the action of the Holy Spirit."[42]

The Spirit seeks to draw members of the faith community more fully and deeply into relationship with Christ. As Bonhoeffer puts it, "Christ can only be grasped *in* the Spirit."[43] And we might add, Christ can only fully grasp us *through* the Spirit. This double grasping suggests that the presence and work of the Spirit is not only comforting and supportive, but also disruptive, bringing us into fuller life with Christ.

Bonhoeffer notes that the Holy Spirit seeks to foster a greater inner awareness and receptivity within us. He explains that members of the church community "are led by the Spirit into solitude" in order to come to a fuller appropriation of their life with God through spiritual practices.[44]

But the work of the Spirit is never only for those in the faith community, for the Spirit of Christ is *for* the redemption and renewal of the whole world. Bonhoeffer makes it clear that "there is no community with Jesus that is not at the same time a *call to service*."[45] Moreover, "the Holy Spirit . . .

---

40. Bonhoeffer, *Works*, vol. 1, 159.
41. Bonhoeffer, *Works*, vol. 9, *Young Bonhoeffer, 1918–1927*, 341.
42. Bonhoeffer, *Works*, vol. 9, 336.
43. Bonhoeffer, *Works*, vol. 9, 340 (emphasis in original).
44. Bonhoeffer, *Works*, vol. 1, *Sanctorum Communio*, 162.
45. Bonhoeffer, *Works*, vol. 15, *Theological Education Underground 1937–1940*, 544 (emphasis in original).

would command loyal service to the gospel," and this loyalty engages all of life, including a life of suffering for the sake of the other.[46]

> *But we are confident, like a mother who knows*
> *the love her son has for all, and we are carriers of that same spirit.*
> *The one that moves us to mercy, recreating and transforming everything,*
> *so that the celebration of life, in which all can dance with joy, does not end.*[47]

---

46. Bonhoeffer, *Works*, vol. 9, *Young Bonhoeffer, 1918–1927*, 268.
47. Carvalhaes, *Liturgies from Below*, 226.

4:6

True Spirit for This Age

Beloved, do not believe every spirit, but test the spirits to see whether they are from God; for many false prophets have gone out into the world. By this you know the Spirit of God: every spirit that confesses that Jesus Christ has come in the flesh is from God.

—1 John 4:1–2

There is little doubt that Bonhoeffer wrestled with what was happening politically in his country as it was being reshaped by Nazi ideology. He also wrestled to discern how the church should respond in the wake of the social distortion and disruption brought about by this ideology.

On the one hand, Bonhoeffer sought to read and reread Scripture in light of the times in which he was living, and this often caused him to read *against* what he saw unfolding in society. At the same time, he sought to read the powers of his age and to bring to Scripture the grave questions and concerns he had about the powers of his time.

In seeking to read both Scripture and the powers, Bonhoeffer rejected the idea that Christianity and the secular world had nothing to do with each other. In writing about secularity, he observes that the human "has become a god against God" and has "made himself [herself] his [her] own creator and judge."[48] He also refutes the idea that the secular world is independent of God, because "the gospel . . . is addressed to the whole world."[49] Moreover, he notes that though the "reign of Jesus Christ over the whole [world] is evidenced and proclaimed" in the church, the church must not keep this good news for itself, but is called to give testimony "about God's redemption in Christ of the world."[50]

48. Bonhoeffer, *Ethics*, 23, 22.
49. Bonhoeffer, *Ethics*, 197.
50. Bonhoeffer, *Ethics*, 199.

Amidst all these competing forces, Bonhoeffer sought to discern the world in terms of its self-assertion and self-autonomy, on the one hand, and also to discern the way in which the goodness and wisdom of God was impacting society, on the other.

In describing this process of discernment, Bonhoeffer observes that the hopes in Germany that were carried by the youth movement (which was enamored by Hitler) did not reflect Christ, for "the spirit of youth is not the Holy Spirit."[51] Moreover, he writes that "the future of the church is not youth itself but rather the Lord Jesus Christ alone."[52] He goes on to say that "the true spirit of the age [*Zeitgeist*] is the Holy Spirit."[53]

There are several important lessons that we can draw from these observations.

First, by stressing the relationship between the Spirit and the word, Bonhoeffer makes the case that we can discern the extent to which movements of the Spirit in society reflect the gospel, or not. As Bonhoeffer insists, "the Spirit can only work through this word" of Christ in the gospel.[54]

Second, by highlighting the dynamic connection between the Spirit and Christ, Bonhoeffer argues that we can speak of the "Spirit of Christ."[55] Christ gives the gift of the Spirit to the believer, and the Spirit brings Christ home to the believer and orchestrates the work of Christ in that person's life. Thus we can look for the footprints of Christ in what is taking place in society.

Third, Bonhoeffer speaks of "Christ existing *as* church-community."[56] While the faith community "lives *by the word alone*," it can only do so because "it has the Spirit."[57] Thus the church is a community of discernment that is shaped by the Spirit. And the task of discernment is concerned with life in the sanctuary as well as life in the world.

Because our world is marked by both beauty and chaos, the spirit of each age needs to be carefully discerned. More is at stake than simply "light" and "darkness," for every movement of change is not necessarily the work of the Holy Spirit.

---

51. Bonhoeffer, *Works*, vol. 12, *Berlin 1932–1933*, 515.
52. Bonhoeffer, *Works*, vol. 12, 515.
53. Bonhoeffer, *Works*, vol. 10, *Barcelona, Berlin, New York 1928–1931*, 529.
54. Bonhoeffer, *Works*, vol. 1, *Sanctorum Communio*, 157.
55. Bonhoeffer, *Works*, vol. 1, 215.
56. Bonhoeffer, *Works*, vol. 1, 190 (emphasis in original).
57. Bonhoeffer, *Works*, vol. 1, 190 (emphasis in original).

Bonhoeffer sees Christ at the very center of everything that is, including "the center of . . . history."[58] But he also sees Christ as the "hidden" one, and he calls us to see the "humiliated Christ" in the world.[59]

> *The law kills, but the Spirit gives life.*
> *Do make yourself known in the life of those without hope,*
> *that in searching the Scriptures, your very Word*
> *would provide encouragement, solace, and empowerment.*
> *Come, Holy Spirit, come.*[60]

---

58. Bonhoeffer, *Christ the Center*, 60.
59. Bonhoeffer, *Christ the Center*, 62.
60. Carvalhaes, *Liturgies from Below*, 283.

5

Sustained by Spiritual Practices

Introduction

BONHOEFFER HAS BEEN IDENTIFIED in a variety of ways—radical, prophet, seer, activist, and saint.[1] But most basically, he was a pastor-theologian who sought to be a Christ follower in a time of great turmoil amidst the midst of the horrors of the holocaust and World War II.

Times of upheaval impact every facet of life, including our inner life and faith. It is easy for our faith to be compromised in such circumstances, and it is also possible to lose our faith altogether.

There is no indication that Bonhoeffer breezed through these momentous times, for he continually wrestled with his faith and unfolding theology, the church and its call to faithful witness, as well as the political issues of his day.

It is also clear that he never saw himself as a self-made hero who could withstand all the onslaughts of his day. Rather, he describes himself during his imprisonment as "restless and longing and sick, like a bird in a cage, . . . trembling with anger at despotism, . . . a contemptible woebegone weakling."[2] Yet during this same season of trial, he also saw himself as "called to obedient and responsible action in faith in exclusive allegiance to God."[3]

---

1. See Haynes, *Bonhoeffer Phenomenon*.
2. Bonhoeffer, *Letters and Papers*, 348.
3. Bonhoeffer, *Letters and Papers*, 5.

Sustained by Spiritual Practices

Because Bonhoeffer saw the whole gestalt of his life as oriented to following Christ in the midst of the church and the world, he practiced a range of spiritual disciplines that sustained him and deepened his commitment to Christ. These disciplines included scriptural study, theological reflection, prayer, meditation, confession, community, friendship, and costly service. As Bonhoeffer wrestled with how he should act in conformity to Christ, who called him to service and suffering in the world, he continually drank at the wells of the biblical narratives and the rich traditions of the church.

Bonhoeffer is well known for his call to live a costly grace and an obedient discipleship in his classic *The Cost of Discipleship*. Yet in living out this call to costly discipleship, he was not seeking to live an austere form of the Christian faith. For even though he stresses that Christ "makes claims upon my entire life,"[4] he celebrates that when we focus on the cross of Christ, we can see that "God will make everything new again."[5] And while he emphasizes that the "Holy Spirit . . . would command loyal service to the gospel,"[6] he rejoices that the Holy Spirit puts "Christ in our hearts, creating faith and hope."[7] He declares that our hope in Christ is our "most sacred treasure."[8]

Moreover, he stresses that the grace of God, while calling us to conversion, also "makes us joyful again and free and sure."[9] This theme of joy is repeated throughout his writings, and he even exclaims that "discipleship *is* joy."[10] He observes that "joy makes us strong."[11] And he declares that joy expresses itself in "gratitude," even when we are "joyous amid tears."[12]

As we engage the spiritual practices that Bonhoeffer drew on for sustenance, we need to keep this theme of joy in front of us, for spiritual practices are not the "grind" of asceticism, nor are they the "fuel" for costly service. Rather, they are an instrument that nurtures joy and beauty in our relationship with God and others.

---

4. Bonhoeffer, *Works*, vol. 10, *Barcelona, Berlin, New York 1928–1931*, 343.
5. Bonhoeffer, *Works*, vol. 10, 358.
6. Bonhoeffer, *Works*, vol. 9, *Young Bonhoeffer, 1918–1927*, 268.
7. Bonhoeffer, *Works*, vol. 1, *Sanctorum Communio*, 165.
8. Bonhoeffer, *Works*, vol. 1, 289.
9. Bonhoeffer, *Works*, vol. 13, *London 1933–1935*, 323.
10. Bonhoeffer, *Works*, vol. 4, *Discipleship*, 40 (emphasis in original).
11. Bonhoeffer, *Works*, vol. 10, *Barcelona, Berlin, New York 1928–1931*, 552.
12. Bonhoeffer, *Works*, vol. 10, 578.

5:1

Prayer

Rejoice in hope, be patient in suffering, persevere in prayer.
—ROMANS 12:12

Bonhoeffer was clearly a pastoral theologian, for themes of pastoral concern are embedded in all of his writings. An emphasis on the practice of prayer also runs as a golden thread throughout his works. While in prison, Bonhoeffer pastorally cared for and prayed for his fellow prisoners, and he also penned liturgical morning and evening prayers for them to use.[13]

Much of Bonhoeffer's discussion about prayer was not only biblical and theological, but also deeply personal. During his imprisonment, he writes to his friend, Eberhard Bethge, "don't forget to pray for me," and he assures Eberhard, "thinking of you with daily prayers."[14] Though he confesses that Eberhard "can pray for me like no one else," he gratefully acknowledges "all the people whose prayers I can count on."[15]

In reflecting on prayer, Bonhoeffer argues that "prayer is the heart of the Christian life" and that "the power of the human being is prayer."[16] Yet he warns that one should not "rely exclusively on one's own prayer," since even "the most personal prayer" belongs "to the church."[17] His point here is that the whole church is a praying community, and Christ, who binds us into a faith community, "is the strength of our prayer."[18]

In reflecting on the church in his time, Bonhoeffer laments that "our age has little room at all for prayer" and that "prayer has become alien to

---

13. Bonhoeffer, *Works*, vol. 8, *Letters and Papers from Prison*, 194–198.
14. Bonhoeffer, *Works*, vol. 8, 517, 519.
15. Bonhoeffer, *Works*, vol. 8, 179, 515.
16. Bonhoeffer, *Works*, vol. 10, *Barcelona, Berlin, New York 1928–1931*, 555, 577.
17. Bonhoeffer, *Works*, vol. 1, *Sanctorum Communio*, 186, 185.
18. Bonhoeffer, *Works*, vol. 10, *Barcelona, Berlin, New York 1928–1931*, 577.

Sustained by Spiritual Practices

us."[19] His call for the renewal of prayer is relevant and pressing in our age as well.

Bonhoeffer acknowledges that the need to recover prayer is not easy for him. He admits that the disturbance of frequent air raids is "leading me . . . back to prayer and the Bible."[20] And somewhat tongue-in-cheek, he confesses, "it takes a crisis to shake us up and drive us into prayer."[21]

In identifying aspects of prayer, Bonhoeffer observes that prayer is, first and foremost, more about listening than talking. He writes that when the heart "has become very still we can call out to the one who hopes to come to us."[22] He notes that in prayer, we need "to become so quiet that we perceive God's word to us."[23]

In another reflection, Bonhoeffer links prayer and action, writing that God "waits for and responds to sincere prayer and responsible action."[24] Elaborating on this connection, he writes, "we can be Christians today in only two ways, through prayer and in doing justice."[25]

Finally, Bonhoeffer accents the call to intercessory prayer. He believes that in "our intercession we can become a Christ to our neighbor."[26] Moreover, he suggests that in praying for others, we "step into the other's place," even "into the other's sin and affliction."[27]

For Bonhoeffer, prayer was neither mere psychological self-talk nor self-therapy, but relational and Christocentric. As we have noted, Bonhoeffer identifies Christ as "the strength of our prayer."[28] Bonhoeffer helps us understand prayer as both a profound experience and a strange and mysterious spiritual discipline, one he describes as an "arcane discipline," not of this world.[29]

> *O Lord Jesus Christ, Son of the Living God,*
> *who . . . was led forth to the pain of the cross*

---

19. Bonhoeffer, *Works*, vol. 10, 576.
20. Bonhoeffer, *Works*, vol. 8, *Letters and Papers*, 204.
21. Bonhoeffer, *Works*, vol. 8, 276.
22. Bonhoeffer, *Works*, vol. 9, *Young Bonhoeffer, 1918–1927*, 512.
23. Bonhoeffer, *Works*, vol. 10, *Barcelona, Berlin, New York 1928–1931*, 577.
24. Bonhoeffer, *Works*, vol. 8, *Letters and Papers from Prison*, 46.
25. Bonhoeffer, *Works*, vol. 8, 389.
26. Bonhoeffer, *Works*, vol. 1, *Sanctorum Communio*, 187.
27. Bonhoeffer, *Works*, vol. 1, 187.
28. Bonhoeffer, *Works*, vol. 10, *Barcelona, Berlin, New York 1928–1931*, 577.
29. Bonhoeffer, *Works*, vol. 8, *Letters and Papers from Prison*, 365.

for the salvation of the world:
we pray that by virtue of your most sacred passion
you would blot out our sins
and mercifully bring us to the glory of your blessedness;
for you are now alive and reign with the Father and the Holy Spirit.[30]

---

30. *Celebrating Common Prayer*, 270.

5:2

Scripture

... when you received the word of God that you heard from us, you accepted it not as a human word but as what it really is, God's word, which is also at work in you ...

—1 Thessalonians 2:13

As a follower of Christ in the midst of an age of turmoil and war, Bonhoeffer continually sought to ground his faith and actions in the gospel and through the guidance of the Spirit. He describes the Christian life as a call to commit to the "risk of placing our lives on Jesus' word."[31] Convinced that "God's revelation in Christ is God's word to the present," he challenges us to embrace Christ's "will and his entire person" to shape our lives, direct our footsteps, and plunge us into the full arena of life "through the Holy Spirit."[32]

Bonhoeffer probed Scripture not to seek information about God or certain theological themes, but with an attentive faith and love so that he might *know* Christ more fully and *live* the life of Christ more truly. He wanted to teach others to read Scripture with the eyes of love and faith so that the church might live as a second "incarnation" of Christ, bringing Christ's redemption, restoration, and healing into the world.

Bonhoeffer's reflective approach to reading Scripture was both christological and attentive to the impulse of the Spirit, both meditative and missional.

Bonhoeffer was neither a detached, abstract thinker nor an impulsive activist. Rather, he was practical and deeply reflective. He perceived that if we made space to listen to God's word deep within our being, we would be empowered to act into life with faith and courage, even if it meant taking

---

31. Bonhoeffer, *Works*, vol. 9, *Young Bonhoeffer, 1918–1927*, 560.
32. Bonhoeffer, *Works*, vol. 10, *Barcelona, Berlin, New York 1928–1931*, 382, 493.

great risks. He writes of the need "to become so quiet that we can perceive God's word to us."[33]

Bonhoeffer warns that a life of Christian discipleship will involve a "strict practice of austerity" so that we will become "more willing and more joyous" in walking this path.[34] To maintain such a life, he speaks of the need to cultivate the "precious gift" of contemplative and meditative practices.[35]

This perspective is crucial, as the practice of meditation is only fruitful if it is a received as a gift of the presence of God. Bonhoeffer explains that the practice of becoming still and entering solitude and engaging in meditative reflection on Scripture "opens for God a space."[36] He laments that we often become "so busy that we can't hear God's voice."[37] But when we open space for God, we receive many gifts from the Spirit.

First, the fruit of meditating on Scripture can become a "healing power promoting renewal" in our lives and in the world.[38]

Second, as we live amidst the issues, questions, and challenges of our time, "daily silent reflection on the word of God" can provide a "constancy" that acts "like a magnet directing all the available powers for ordering our life towards its pole."[39] Rather than experiencing confusion and disorientation in times of turmoil, we can act meaningfully by drinking from the "pure deep water" of meditation, which not only helps us, but also "serves the Most High."[40]

Finally, Bonhoeffer observes that reflecting on Scripture "as it applies to me" can produce a "crystallization of all that brings inner and outer order to my life."[41] This insight brings contemplation and action, prayer and service into one arc of faithful and costly discipleship, where we seek to follow Christ into the fray of life, with all its beauty and pain.

> *Blessed Lord,*
> *who caused all holy Scriptures*
> *to be written for our learning:*

---

33. Bonhoeffer, *Works*, vol. 10, 577.
34. Bonhoeffer, *Works*, vol. 4, *Discipleship*, 158.
35. Bonhoeffer, *Works*, vol. 16, *Conspiracy and Imprisonment 1940–1945*, 254.
36. Bonhoeffer, *Works*, vol, 16, 254.
37. Bonhoeffer, *Works*, vol. 9, *Young Bonhoeffer, 1918–1927*, 512.
38. Bonhoeffer, *Works*, vol. 16, *Conspiracy and Imprisonment 1940–1945*, 255.
39. Bonhoeffer, *Works*, vol, 16, 254.
40. Bonhoeffer, *Works*, vol, 16, 254.
41. Bonhoeffer, *Works*, vol. 16, 254.

Sustained by Spiritual Practices

help us to hear them,
to read, mark, learn and inwardly digest them
that, through patience and the comfort of your holy word,
we may embrace and for ever hold fast
the hope of eternal life.[42]

---

42. *Celebrating Common Prayer*, 422.

5:3

Faith

Now it is evident that no one is justified before God by the law; for "The one who is righteous will live by faith."

—GALATIANS 3:11

Bonhoeffer believed that humans are called to orient the whole of our lives to God and that we can only understand ourselves "*through* God."[43] Such an orientation has many dimensions, but it reminds us that our understanding is only partial and can be distorted by our biases and cultural blinkers. As Bonhoeffer puts it, we can never fully understand God, ourselves, or the world around us without faith, for "the highest form of existence is faith," and faith in Christ "is only true in discipleship."[44]

Bonhoeffer makes it clear that the genesis of faith does not begin with the self, but by "hearing the Word of God."[45] Moreover, "the act of receiving this word of God" in faith occurs with "God in his revelation as the Holy Spirit."[46] Thus faith begins as God draws near to us, for "the human being can never capture God in his [her] thoughts."[47]

Bonhoeffer also stresses that the outworking of our faith is a life of obedience and discipleship in following Christ, which issues forth in a "faithful existence,"[48] a way of life—or *"habitus"*—that will be sustained by spiritual practices.[49] Bonhoeffer describes this *"habitus"* as being faithful to the church, bearing one's own and others' burdens, engaging Scripture,

---

43. Bonhoeffer, *Works*, vol. 12, *Berlin 1932–1933*, 219 (emphasis in original).
44. Bonhoeffer, *Works*, vol. 12, 229, 259.
45. Bonhoeffer, *Works*, vol. 12, 227.
46. Bonhoeffer, *Works*, vol. 10, *Barcelona, Berlin, New York 1928–1931*, 459.
47. Bonhoeffer, *Works*, vol. 12, *Berlin 1932–1933*, 224.
48. Bonhoeffer, *Works*, vol. 12, 222.
49. Bonhoeffer, *Works*, vol. 12, 231 (emphasis in original).

living prayerfully, practicing meditation, exploring one's conscience, and serving others.[50]

Bonhoeffer does not suggest that living this life of faith will be easy, constant, or automatic. We have a sure foundation, for "God set the beginning once through his forgiving and renewing word in Jesus Christ."[51] But this initial conversion needs to recaptured and repeated, for "faith and obedience live out of remembrance and repetition."[52] Thus we each need to hear "God's daily new word addressed to me."[53]

Bonhoeffer describes the life of faith as a dynamic attentiveness to God, where we "open the doors of our hearts to the Master."[54] This life involves prayer and the constant plea, "*Veni creator spiritus.*"[55] It also involves a commitment to community, where we live our life together as a "sign of the gracious presence of the triune God."[56] Finally, it involves service in the world, for the church lives as "the presence of God in the world."[57]

For Bonhoeffer, the life of faith is "justified by grace alone" and is rooted in the "death and resurrection of Christ."[58] Simply put, the "Christian life is the life of Christ."[59]

But our life in Christ takes us into the world to live a life of prayer, witness, and service. Bonhoeffer writes that "in Christ the reality of God entered the reality of the world."[60] Moreover, he says that the Christian "belonging wholly to Christ . . . stands at the same time wholly in the world."[61] Thus the Christian has faith in what God will *yet* do in our world for its healing and transformation.

> *Therefore, anything that creates has life,*
> *for if it did not have life, it could not create.*
> *Thus, faith that is generative is alive,*

---

50. Bonhoeffer, *Works*, vol. 12, 232.
51. Bonhoeffer, *Works*, vol. 15, *Theological Education Underground 1937–1940*, 497.
52. Bonhoeffer, *Works*, vol. 15, 518.
53. Bonhoeffer, *Works*, vol. 15, 517.
54. Bonhoeffer, *Works*, vol. 9, *Young Bonhoeffer, 1918–1927*, 512.
55. Bonhoeffer, *Works*, vol. 9, 298.
56. Bonhoeffer, *Life Together*, 20.
57. Bonhoeffer, *Works*, vol. 12, *Berlin 1932–1933*, 263.
58. Bonhoeffer, *Ethics*, 121.
59. Bonhoeffer, *Ethics*, 122.
60. Bonhoeffer, *Ethics*, 197.
61. Bonhoeffer, *Ethics*, 198.

*because it is animated by the life of love . . .
And in the same way, idle faith is not alive,
because it lacks the life of love.*[62]

---

62. From St. Anselm of Canterbury (c. 1033–1109). Quoted in Ringma and Alexander, eds., *Of Martyrs, Monks, and Mystics*, 68.

5:4

Friendship

*Some friends play at friendship
but a true friend sticks closer than one's nearest of kin.*

—Proverbs 18:24

Bonhoeffer was deeply tied to his family, friends, intentional community, and the church. He nurtured friendships with Eberhard Bethge, Bishop George Bell in the UK, and Ruth von Kleist-Retzow, among many others.

In a letter, Bonhoeffer celebrates his close friendship with Eberhard, thanking him for his patience, advice, and prayers, and observing that "friendship is . . . a rather extraordinary joy for human life."[63] Bonhoeffer did not understand friendship in a superficial or functional way, for as he confesses to Eberhard, "I wish that we might continue to have in each other the person we can trust unreservedly, without limit."[64] He emphasizes that friendship is part of God's purposes for humanity, noting that all relationships are "from God to God," including "the *relationship of friendship*."[65]

While Bonhoeffer gives practical advice on the art of friendship, he grounds his reflections theologically. Because God exists as a community of mutuality and friendship, we are called to reflect this trinitarian reality in our relationships. Within this broad theological frame, Bonhoeffer makes the point that "God created human beings to complement each other," which includes the relationship between "friend and friend."[66] More generally, Bonhoeffer points out that "God intended for us to live among nations, families, and friendships."[67]

---

63. Bonhoeffer, *Works*, vol. 10, *Barcelona, Berlin, New York 1928–1931*, 136.
64. Bonhoeffer, *Works*, vol. 8, *Letters and Papers from Prison*, 511.
65. Bonhoeffer, *Works*, vol. 1, *Sanctorum Communio*, 95 (emphasis in original).
66. Bonhoeffer, *Works*, vol. 10, *Barcelona, Berlin, New York 1928–1931*, 538.
67. Bonhoeffer, *Works*, vol. 9, *Young Bonhoeffer, 1918–1927*, 535.

Bonhoeffer makes it clear that the dynamic of friendship—the ability to love, be loyal, forgive, and express other virtues—"has its basis in God."[68] For the power of God's love in Christ through the Spirit reorients and empowers a person of faith to live in the way of Christ, who was a friend to all humanity and the world because he gave his life for the redemption and healing of all.

In Bonhoeffer's reflections on the practices of friendship, he recognizes that friendship is both a gift and a challenging endeavor. He writes that it is "easier to immerse oneself in the spirit of a school class than in that of friendship."[69] He explains that friendship is more difficult because being a good friend involves the willingness "to sacrifice some of your own will" and "some of your own wishes."[70]

Bonhoeffer is confident that "no friendship endures without . . . forgiving, nonjudgmental love."[71] Because of Christ's self-giving and vicarious suffering for others, those who follow him are called to be committed to "vicarious representative action"[72] for all, including the neighbor. Bonhoeffer writes about being willing and "able to bow beneath the claim of one's neighbor in the spirit of passionate sacrifice."[73] Surely this must also be true with friends.

While Bonhoeffer stresses that we are part of the body of Christ as a faith community, and we are joined to one another in mutual relationships, he also asserts that we must still maintain our individual identity. He argues that it is "through the call of Jesus" that humans "become individuals. . . . It is no choice of their own . . . : it is Christ who makes them individuals by calling them."[74] And he observes, "We are separated from one another by an unbridgeable gulf of otherness and strangeness," and no attempt at "natural association or emotional or spiritual union" will undo this gulf.[75]

Yet Christ the Mediator "stands between us," and we can only be connected with others "through him."[76] Bonhoeffer elaborates that because

---

68. Bonhoeffer, *Works*, vol. 10, *Barcelona, Berlin, New York 1928–1931*, 554.
69. Bonhoeffer, *Works*, vol. 1, *Sanctorum Communio*, 100.
70. Bonhoeffer, *Works*, vol. 10, *Barcelona, Berlin, New York 1928–1931*, 554.
71. Bonhoeffer, *Works*, vol. 10, 499.
72. Bonhoeffer, *Works*, vol. 1, *Sanctorum Communio*, 156.
73. Bonhoeffer, *Works*, vol. 10, *Barcelona, Berlin, New York 1928–1931*, 534.
74. Bonhoeffer, *Cost of Discipleship*, 84.
75. Bonhoeffer, *Cost of Discipleship*, 87.
76. Bonhoeffer, *Cost of Discipleship*, 88.

Sustained by Spiritual Practices

"Christ the Mediator" stands "between father and son, husband and wife, the individual and the nation"—and thus between friend and friend—we can make true contact with others "through him, through his word, and through our following him."[77] All of this points toward great freedom in relationships, not control.

Almighty God, you have given us your only-begotten Son
to take our nature upon him . . . [and] made children by adoption and grace,
may [we] daily be renewed by your Holy Spirit.[78]

---

77. Bonhoeffer, *Cost of Discipleship*, 86.
78. *Celebrating Common Prayer*, 350.

5:5

Vulnerability and Confession

If we say that we have no sin, we deceive ourselves, and the truth is not in us. If we confess our sins, he who is faithful and just will forgive us our sins and cleanse us from all unrighteousness.

—1 John 1:8–9

There is nothing elitist or triumphalistic in Bonhoeffer's theology and spirituality. Instead, he promotes a spirituality of vulnerability as we seek to follow Christ—the redeemer, icon of the new humanity, and suffering servant.

We express our vulnerability through our obedient posture before God and by sharing and participating in the faith community, being willing to admit failure and fault, and committing to serve our neighbors.

To live out a vulnerable faith requires costly grace, not the cheap grace of "forgiveness without . . . repentance" and "communion without confession."[79] Bonhoeffer argues that such "cheap grace" is "without discipleship, . . . without the cross, . . . without Jesus Christ, living and incarnate."[80]

In the fascist world of Bonhoeffer's time, might was right and false ideology trumped truth. Yet Bonhoeffer sought to promote the truth of the Living Word, Jesus Christ, who calls us to tell the truth about ourselves and our nation.

In telling the truth about ourselves, Bonhoeffer emphasizes that all followers of Christ should be marked by God's bounteous grace and the humility of confession. Telling the truth about ourselves is based on the "cross," which is "God's truth about us," and in this place, our "sin has been uncovered, and forgiven by Jesus."[81]

---

79. Bonhoeffer, *Cost of Discipleship*, 36.
80. Bonhoeffer, *Cost of Discipleship*, 36.
81. Bonhoeffer, *Cost of Discipleship*, 125.

Sustained by Spiritual Practices

Though Bonhoeffer sees the church as a faith community of forgiveness, he stresses that we are called to practice confession to God and also in the presence of another Christian. He writes that in the "confession of sin before another Christian, the flesh dies together with its pride."[82]

This form of confession, Bonhoeffer insists, "is the God-given remedy for self-deception and self-indulgence," as it identifies us with the shame and death of Christ.[83] Moreover, after hearing the word of absolution spoken to us by a member of the faith community, on Christ's behalf, we are free to rise with Christ in newness of life.

Bonhoeffer is deeply concerned that unconfessed sin has an inordinate power over us, as it draws us into isolation, which fractures the lived reality of the community in Christ. When we engage in the practice of confession, however, we abandon our wrongdoing, and we give our "heart to God," where we find "the forgiveness of . . . sin in the fellowship of Jesus Christ" that we share with our brothers and sisters in the faith.[84] When we fail to live in this way, however, Bonhoeffer insists that "we refuse to bear the Cross," for "we are ashamed to take upon ourselves the shameful death of the sinner in confession."[85]

While Bonhoeffer situates his discussion of confession in preparation for partaking in Holy Communion, confession does not need to be limited in this way. It is always appropriate for Christians to share joys, sorrows, and the confession of sins with one another in the faith community. To live in this vulnerable way composes the Christian life into a melody of joy.

By the mystery of your holy incarnation; by your birth,
childhood, and obedience; by your baptism, fasting, and temptation,
Good Lord, deliver us.
By your agony and trial; by your cross and passion;
by your precious death and burial,
Good Lord, deliver us.
By your mighty resurrection; by your glorious ascension;
and by your sending of the Holy Spirit,
Good Lord, deliver us.[86]

---

82. Bonhoeffer, *Works*, vol. 4, *Discipleship*, 270.
83. Bonhoeffer, *Cost of Discipleship*, 260.
84. Bonhoeffer, *Life Together*, 112.
85. *Life Together*, 114.
86. *Celebrating Common Prayer*, 250.

5:6

Suffering

When we cry, "Abba! Father!" it is that very Spirit bearing witness with our spirit that we are children of God, and if children, then heirs, heirs of God and joint heirs with Christ—if, in fact, we suffer with him so that we may also be glorified with him.

—ROMANS 8:15–17

Bonhoeffer lived during a time when he was surrounded by all sorts of challenges and difficulties, and nothing seemed to come out right. Hitler's madness continued. Bonhoeffer's illegal seminary was closed. The Confessing Church was in crisis. Personal faith was under threat.

Writing of the Confessing Church, Bonhoeffer notes that it "lost its faith-awakening and . . . its discerning power" and was in a state of "paralysis."[87] To sustain personal faith, Bonhoeffer speaks of the need for "fervent prayer," to look more to "God's Spirit," and to live in the hope that "God will give his witness anew into our hearts."[88]

In this setting, Bonhoeffer asks, "how much personal sacrifice" are we called to make?[89] To put this another way, how much suffering are we called to bear?

Throughout his writings, Bonhoeffer explores various dimensions of suffering—our identification with the suffering Christ, our identification with the suffering of those in the body of Christ, and our vicarious experience of those who are suffering in our world.

Bonhoeffer observes that "suffering and rejection express in summary form the cross of Jesus."[90] Moreover, as followers of Christ, he insists

---

87. Bonhoeffer, *Works*, vol. 15, *Theological Education Underground 1937–1940*, 31, 32.
88. Bonhoeffer, *Works*, vol. 15, 35, 40, 35.
89. Bonhoeffer, *Works*, vol. 15, 30.
90. Bonhoeffer, *Works*, vol. 4, *Discipleship*, 85.

that we will need to bear the shape of his cross, for "Jesus has to make it clear and unmistakable to his disciples that the need to suffer now applies to them, too."[91]

Yet Bonhoeffer does not see this call to suffering as a distressing reality, but rather a form of identification with Christ, which he accepts as a "grace and joy."[92]

In this section, we will explore the rich tapestry of Bonhoeffer's discussion of suffering.

First, Bonhoeffer emphasizes that God is continually seeking both to sustain and challenge those in the faith community. While the church should raise its voice in protest about the injustices happening in society, Christians will also experience "God's protest against us," which may include suffering.[93] Bonhoeffer insists that "suffering leads to the recognition of sin and thus a turning to God," and therefore suffering is a form of purgation.[94]

Second, Bonhoeffer argues that Christians should not live apart from the world, but "must experience the sufferings of this world," because Christ is *for the* healing and transformation of the world.[95] Bonhoeffer makes it clear that we cannot redeem the world "by our own deeds and sufferings."[96] Yet he also insists that we are called to share in "Christ's large-heartedness" for the world and to respond with "sympathy and action."[97]

Third, Bonhoeffer stresses that our engagement with the world is fundamental to our discipleship, for "the cultivation of a Christian inner life, untouched by the world," is in fact "tragicomical."[98] As he explains, the Christian "belonging wholly to Christ . . . stands at the same time wholly in the world."[99] Moreover, the community of faith is called to "struggle . . . against the essential character of the fallen world itself," and this will require us to "give [our] life in sacrifice."[100]

---

91. Bonhoeffer, *Works*, vol. 4, 85.
92. Bonhoeffer, *Works*, vol. 4, 89.
93. Bonhoeffer, *Works*, vol. 12, *Berlin 1932–1933*, 441.
94. Bonhoeffer, *Works*, vol. 15, *Theological Education Underground 1937–1940*, 407.
95. Bonhoeffer, *Works*, vol. 15, 407.
96. Bonhoeffer, *Letters and Papers from Prison*, 14.
97. Bonhoeffer, *Letters and Papers*, 14.
98. Bonhoeffer, *Ethics*, 198.
99. Bonhoeffer, *Ethics*, 198.
100. Bonhoeffer, *Ethics*, 164, 165.

Thus as disciples of Christ, we must suffer the realities of the world along with others—but we do so sustained by prayer and by the joy of our identification with Christ.

> *God of grace and goodness,*
> *who made us body and spirit*
> *that our work and faith may be one:*
> *may we, by our life and worship,*
> *join in your labour to bring forth a new creation*
> *in justice, love, and truth;*
> *through Jesus our Redeemer.*[101]

---

101. *Celebrating Common Prayer*, 73.

6

Resisting the Powers

Introduction

WE ARE ALL SHAPED by the world through our socialization and inculturation. Marked by finitude and historicity, we participate in the life of the world, and so we experience all of its sustenance and beauty as well as its brokenness and dysfunctionality.

But Christians have a unique relationship to the world in that they see it as God's world, and they also see it as being marked by idolatry. In other words, they see both the folly and woundedness of the world as well as its goodness. Moreover, they see both its progress and its limitations in light of God's purposes and final future.

In light of this unique relationship, Christians are *part* of the world, but also *apart* from the world. Shaped by the narratives of Scripture and committed to follow the way of Christ, they see the world differently and seek to inhabit it in a different way. This, in some way, makes them misfits within the broader culture.

Yet being misfits has nothing to do with abandoning the world, but rather calls Christians to seek to bless and heal our world so that it may reflect more of God's goodness and shalom. In seeking to bless and heal the world with God's shalom, those in the faith community pray for our world and actively engage to renew and transform it.

This positive engagement has two dimensions. The first is the *annunciation* of good news, which is God's creational care for and sustenance of the world, God's redemption in Christ, the renewing work of the Spirit, and the calling of the faith community to serve the world.

The second dimension is the *denunciation* of all that has become distorted and oppressive in the world. When societal powers—ideologies, institutions, and religious forces—become idolatrous, they need to be confronted and resisted. And when the church becomes bad news to the world, it needs to be exposed and challenged.

Bonhoeffer resisted Hitler's distorted leadership and political ideology, and he worked for change when that distorted ideology began to impact the leadership of the church, the safety of the Jewish community, and the nation as a whole. Throughout his writings, he provides a theological vision for resisting the powers.

This vision is rooted in Bonhoeffer's assertion that Christ is "the *center* and strength of the Bible, of the church, and of theology, but also of humanity, of reason, of justice, and of culture."[1] This understanding opens up "the wide extent of [the church's] responsibility" under God, towards the world.[2] For "in Jesus Christ the reality of God entered into the reality of the world" to bring about its renewal, and therefore the church is called to do the same.[3] While the world in its worldliness may wish to live independently of God, Bonhoeffer's redemptive theology highlights how "the whole reality of the world is already drawn in into Christ."[4]

Thus the task of the church is not "the cultivation of a Christian inner life, untouched by the world," but rather to pray, proclaim, and work for the renewal and restoration of *all* dimensions of life so that they reflect the shalom of God.[5] To take up this task, we need to be deeply impacted by the gospel so that we can discern what is good in our world that needs to strengthened—along with what is not good in our world, which needs to be resisted, challenged, and transformed.

Though Bonhoeffer took up this challenge amidst the darkest of times, he believed that the cross of Christ would open our gaze to behold "when God will make everything new again."[6] And such vision "will

---

1. Bonhoeffer, *Ethics*, 58 (emphasis in original).
2. Bonhoeffer, *Ethics*, 60–61.
3. Bonhoeffer, *Ethics*, 192.
4. Bonhoeffer, *Ethics*, 195.
5. Bonhoeffer, *Ethics*, 198.
6. Bonhoeffer, *Works*, vol. 10, *Barcelona, Berlin, New York 1928–1931*, 358.

cause grace and compassion to radiate over the dark guilt of our century and the human race."[7]

---

7. Bonhoeffer, *Works*, vol. 10, 359.

6:1

Keeping Step with a Different Drummer

But it is God who establishes us with you in Christ and has anointed us, by putting his seal on us and giving us his Spirit in our hearts as a first installment.

—2 Corinthians 1:21–22

Many family and social factors are at play regarding one's participation in the life of the church. Bonhoeffer's mother had a pietist background, but the family was not overtly religious. Yet at a very young age, Bonhoeffer declared that he wished to study theology and work for change in the church.

Bonhoeffer admits that initially, his orientation was "more academic."[8] But then he speaks of gaining an "inner clarity and honesty by really starting to take the Sermon on the Mount seriously."[9] As a consequence, Bonhoeffer speaks of a radical reorientation, "where all human desires, ideas, and ways, were crossed by God's way."[10] After such an encounter with Christ, he writes that life becomes "one great act of trust in God," and he argues that our belief in God will "take away our faith in all other powers."[11]

In these reflections, Bonhoeffer reveals that being *captivated* by Christ is quite different from simply *believing* in Christ. When Christ becomes the central orientation of our life, we not only seek to grow in relationship with God and participate in the faith community, but we also begin to see all of life and its institutions in a new light.

For Bonhoeffer, following the gospel and the way of Christ became a new basis for his life, the focus of his ministry, and the lens through which he interpreted everything that was happening in society during his time.

---

8. Bonhoeffer, *Works*, vol. 13, *London 1933–1935*, 284.
9. Bonhoeffer, *Works*, vol. 13, 284–285.
10. Bonhoeffer, *Works*, vol. 13, 400.
11. Bonhoeffer, *Works*, vol. 13, 405.

He believed that the more fully he could be grasped *by* Christ, the more truly he could see God's purposes for the world in restoring all that had been perverted to what it was intended to be. Bonhoeffer wrestled with the relationship between faith and obedience in following Christ and challenged the faith community to ask, "how can we live the Christian life in the modern world?"[12]

In wrestling with this question, he came to the startling conclusion that living the Christian life does not guarantee us certainty, comfort, and blessing, but rather "absolute insecurity."[13] For as we pledge "allegiance to the suffering Christ,"[14] we will be moved to give ourselves to our neighbors as we live out "their claim on ourselves."[15] In this way, we live the "breach" that Christ brings in relation to our natural social existence.[16]

To follow the way of Christ in society, we must live the whole of our life by keeping step with a different drummer. This has nothing to do with being negative about our social reality and institutions, but with bringing the vision and way of Christ into all areas of life, including the economic, political, and artistic.

In order to live this way, we first need to be impacted by the living Christ through the Spirit. Second, we must be deeply shaped by the biblical narratives. Third, we need to receive the insight to see life in all its goodness and all its dysfunctionality in the light of Christ. Finally, we need the courage to act and work for change, even at great cost to ourselves.

> *And we give thanks*
> *for all that holds us together in our humanity;*
> *that binds us to all that live and have lived,*
> *who have cried and are crying,*
> *who hunger and are thirsty,*
> *who pine for justice,*
> *and who hold out for the time [that] is coming.*[17]

---

12. Bonhoeffer, *Cost of Discipleship*, 47.
13. Bonhoeffer, *Cost of Discipleship*, 49.
14. Bonhoeffer, *Cost of Discipleship*, 80.
15. Bonhoeffer, *Cost of Discipleship*, 67.
16. Bonhoeffer, *Cost of Discipleship*, 85.
17. Morley, ed., *Bread of Tomorrow*, 84.

6:2

Discerning When to Say, "No"

But Peter and the apostles answered, "We must obey God rather than any human authority. The God of our ancestors raised up Jesus, whom you killed by hanging him on a tree."

—Acts 5:29–30

Those who are in power will often go to great lengths to justify whatever they are seeking to accomplish in society. Sometimes this involves pressuring people to conform to societal institutions and expectations, even if it means turning a deaf ear to injustice and abuse. Whereas some people are driven by a desire to fit in and conform to the major contours of society, others are far more "edgy" and questioning. Within these extremes, it can be challenging to live a life that is both *affirming* and *critical*.

We can look to Bonhoeffer as a model, for he lived this dialectic as he affirmed the role of government, but criticized Hitler's governance. He was positive about the role of the church in the purposes of God for humanity, but critical of the church's conformity to Nazi ideology. He affirmed scholarly approaches to studying Scripture, but was critical of the failure of many Christians to listen obediently to Scripture. Finally, he affirmed faith in Christ, but criticized conversion without costly discipleship in the way of Christ.

Thus Bonhoeffer studied the world as well as his time and responded with both a "yes" and a "no." In *Ethics*, he points out that some Christians only look towards the "ultimate"[18]—God's final purposes—while neglecting present-life realities. At the same time, other Christians only focus on the "penultimate"[19]—present-day concerns—while failing to live out God's loving concern for the whole world, as it is expressed through the incarnation

18. Bonhoeffer, *Ethics*, 126.
19. Bonhoeffer, *Ethics*, 127.

("the love of God for His creation"), the crucifixion ("the judgement of God upon all flesh"), and the resurrection ("God's will for a new world").[20]

In living out God's passion for a renewed world, we need to say "No" to the deforming ways of culture. Yet such refusals should not be reactive, but the fruit of the Spirit, which will prompt us to question what is lacking and unjust in our world and then to discern how we might work to rectify it.

Bonhoeffer's most persistent critique is the weakening of the gospel, which results in "cheap grace" rather than "costly grace."[21] In his now-classic *The Cost of Discipleship,* he proposes that "grace and discipleship are inseparable."[22] In critiquing "abstract Christology," he speaks of the call to follow "the living Christ."[23] He also rejects the spiritualization of the gospel or seeking a life of "inner detachment," insisting instead Christians are called to live with self-giving relinquishment and generosity in the way of Christ.[24] He refutes the gospel of prosperity, noting that the "cross [is] laid on every Christian."[25] And he criticizes world-denying forms of Christianity, calling Christians to embrace a "genuine love of the world" by giving themselves to living out "the love wherewith God loved [the world] in Jesus Christ."[26]

Moreover, Bonhoeffer rejects the all-too-ready Christian justification of violence and war, suggesting instead that we are called to "renounce all violence and tumult."[27] Yet he also upholds that we can't make nonresistance a principle for secular life, since such a stance denies God's call for the "preservation of the world."[28]

Finally, Bonhoeffer criticizes all forms of Christianity that neglect spiritual practices, arguing that prayer is "the supreme instance of the hidden character of the Christian life."[29]

---

20. Bonhoeffer, *Ethics,* 130.
21. Bonhoeffer, *Cost of Discipleship,* 36–38.
22. Bonhoeffer, *Cost of Discipleship,* 38.
23. Bonhoeffer, *Cost of Discipleship,* 50.
24. Bonhoeffer, *Cost of Discipleship,* 70.
25. Bonhoeffer, *Cost of Discipleship,* 79.
26. Bonhoeffer, *Cost of Discipleship,* 88.
27. Bonhoeffer, *Cost of Discipleship,* 102.
28. Bonhoeffer, *Cost of Discipleship,* 130.
29. Bonhoeffer, *Cost of Discipleship,* 146.

From all of the above, we can see that for Bonhoeffer, the Christian life involves wrestling with the issues of our day and grappling with our understanding of what is happening in our world. Such questioning will require ongoing discernment, along with the faith and courage to say "No" when necessary, so that God's most generous and gracious "Yes," in Christ, might flourish in our world.

> *Give us clear eyes*
> *to see the world as it is,*
> *and ourselves*
> *and all people as they are;*
> *but give us hope to go on believing*
> *in what you intend*
> *us all to be.*[30]

---

30. Morley, ed., *Bread for Tomorrow*, 62.

6:3

Living the Christ Reality

He has told you, O mortal, what is good;
and what does the Lord require of you
but to do justice, and to love kindness,
and to walk humbly with your God?

—Micah 6:8

We are all shaped by the ways we have been socialized, the values we hold, and the particular choices we have made. But to live well, our life must have some coherence, for we are not merely a collection of disjointed fragments pieced together from our imaginations, thoughts, and values. Yet amidst this coherence, there will always be tensions and mystery.

As Christians, we seek to live out our particular story within the frame of God's narrative arc as it is conveyed in the biblical stories. The narrative of Scripture calls us to a whole new way of being, challenging us continually to live a life of repentance, growth, and transformation as we attune ourselves to its melody line. The biblical narrative celebrates God's creative and redemptive activity, which is most fully revealed in Christ, who came to redeem all that sin brought into the world and to usher the whole creation into God's final future, where all things will be restored.

As Bonhoeffer makes clear, in "Jesus Christ the reality of God entered into the reality of the world," and the good that is yet to come into our world is also a "reality in Jesus Christ."[31] As Christians, we are joined by faith to Jesus Christ, and we are called to continue to bring the good news of God's love through Christ into the world. In this way, we participate in both "the reality of God" and "the reality of the world."[32]

---

31. Bonhoeffer, *Ethics*, 192.
32. Bonhoeffer, *Ethics*, 192.

As we live God's narrative in the world, we will encounter other ideological, political, and cultural narratives that might also claim to be good news. Yet we cannot simply leave the world to its own narratives and its own authority. For as Bonhoeffer points out, the world does not exist "independently of the revelation of God in Christ," and "the whole reality of the world is already drawn into Christ."[33]

Thus as we engage these other narratives in our world, we will need to discern the places where humanity is seeking to be "like God," thereby becoming what Bonhoeffer describes as "a god against God."[34] These narratives need to be redeemed by the narrative of God's love for the world as it is expressed through the person and work of Christ. This storied event is not merely an idea or an ideal, for it continues through the inspiration of the ever-present Holy Spirit, who reorients us, sustains us, and empowers us to live as a sign, servant, and sacrament of the reign of God in the world.

As we seek to live the Christ narrative in the world, we need to resist any impulse to become isolationist, elitist, critical, or condemning. For the Christ narrative tells the story of a mother's love for a wayward child, and the heartbeat of this story is prayer and costly care so that all of life—the personal, social, and institutional—will be redeemed through healing, forgiveness, shalom, justice, human flourishing, and societal harmony to the glory of God.

Exuberant Spirit of God,
bursting with the brightness of flame
into the coldness of our lives
to warm us with a passion for justice and beauty.
Exuberant Spirit of God,
sweeping us out of the dusty corners of our apathy
to breathe vitality
into our struggles for change.[35]

---

33. Bonhoeffer, *Ethics*, 195.
34. Bonhoeffer, *Ethics*, 23.
35. Morley, ed., *Bread for Tomorrow*, 129.

6:4

Faith Steeled by Courage

Be strong and of good courage. Do not be afraid or dismayed.
—1 Chronicles 22:13b

Bonhoeffer speaks clearly about the power of the Christian faith in the risen Christ—and also about his conviction that a life of following Christ will involve great difficulty and uncertainty. As he writes from prison, "we are only too familiar with life's anxieties and with all the other destructive effects of prolonged personal insecurity."[36]

Though he acknowledges that such insecurity can easily lead to "resignation" or "pious escapism," he suggests that another way is possible, for Christians are called to live "in faith and responsibility as though there were to be a great future."[37] Yet this hope is not a mere pipe dream, for it should lead us to caring action as we seek to participate in "Christ's large-heartedness."[38]

Bonhoeffer explains that our "Christian hope of resurrection" sends us "back to [our] life on earth in a wholly new way."[39] This "new way" is possible because Christ is not only the center of each individual Christian life, but also "the center" of all the dimensions of life.[40] Thus Bonhoeffer emphasizes that we should "speak of God not at the boundaries [of life] but at the center, not in weakness but in strength."[41]

To live from this center during difficult times is a great challenge, particularly when things are going badly in both society and the church.

---

36. Bonhoeffer, *Letters and Papers*, 16.
37. Bonhoeffer, *Letters and Papers*, 15.
38. Bonhoeffer, *Letters and Papers*, 14.
39. Bonhoeffer, *Letters and Papers*, 336–337.
40. Bonhoeffer, *Letters and Papers*, 312.
41. Bonhoeffer, *Letters and Papers*, 282.

In addition to the challenges Bonhoeffer faced in the Nazification of the church and the German nation, he also encountered a "failure of church leadership" in the Confessing Church (which had rejected Hitler's program of Nazification).[42] During this season, he speaks of "hearts and hands that are tired."[43]

In such weary times, we cannot give up, but must continue to act with courage as we seek to live in faith and hope. Bonhoeffer argues that "one cannot believe without courage," because faith involves action, and action requires courage.[44]

Yet Bonhoeffer also speaks of a "fearful courage" that is marked by "trumpet blowing."[45] Such displays of pseudo-faith are pompous and ostentatious, for true courage requires quiet focus and determination. Such courage is not something we can work up within ourselves, for we can only receive it as God's gift from a deep place within us.

True courage often arises in unexpected times, "when one after another all the things our life depends on are taken away," and we are most vulnerable.[46] During such times, we can take courage in "God . . . coming near to us."[47]

Such hopeful courage is needed when we have to walk out of step with the dominant culture that distorts God's shalom so that we can follow the long arc of the road to justice. Such faithful courage is needed to resist the idolatrous powers of our age and raise a prophetic voice in protest.

Bonhoeffer makes it clear that all true courage is rooted in seeking God and God's will so that we can bring about the purposes of God in the world. Thus Bonhoeffer invites the whole faith community "to have the courage to be *alone* with God as Lord."[48] When we are encountered by the Lord, we can enter the fray of life as those who adhere "to the person of Christ"[49] and who can "always see other men [women] as brethren [sisters] to whom Christ comes."[50]

---

42. Bonhoeffer, *Works*, vol. 15, *Theological Education Underground 1937–1940*, 417.
43. Bonhoeffer, *Works*, vol. 15, 418.
44. Bonhoeffer, *Works*, vol. 9, *Young Bonhoeffer, 1918–1927*, 506.
45. Bonhoeffer, *Works*, vol. 12, *Berlin 1932–1933*, 439.
46. Bonhoeffer, *Works*, vol. 12, 459.
47. Bonhoeffer, *Works*, vol. 12, 459.
48. Bonhoeffer, *Works*, vol. 12, 463.
49. Bonhoeffer, *Cost of Discipleship*, 49.
50. Bonhoeffer, *Cost of Discipleship*, 163.

Resisting the Powers

O God,
pillar of fire and pentecostal flame,
we confess
our lack of inner fire
for your justice to be done,
your peace shared on earth.
Forgive us . . .
we long for healing; we choose your life.[51]

---

51. Morley, ed., *Bread of Tomorrow*, 158.

6:5

Sharing in Christ's Suffering

Share in suffering like a good soldier in Christ.
—2 Timothy 2:3

While there is much in life that is so good, and there is much to be thankful for, life also has its challenges, and we all experience loss and disappointment, regardless of where we live. Not even the rich lead a charmed life!

Yet some suffer more than others. Despite democratic forms of government and welfare policies in the West, some people have a very poor quality of life. And in dictatorial countries with weak social institutions, many people suffer from underemployment, marginalization, exploitation, and abuse.

The Christian tradition emphasizes caring for the poor and helping the needy, and Bonhoeffer's particular heart for the disadvantaged was spawned by his relationship with Christ. As a theologian, he was never an armchair scholar, but always sought to ground his faith in a life of action. Moreover, he sought to emulate the central motif revealed in the biblical narrative, which is that God, in Christ, followed a way of humiliation and suffering in order to heal a broken and wounded humanity.

Bonhoeffer makes it clear that "only the sufferings of Christ are a means of atonement" and that Christ had "to bear the sins of others" so that there could be forgiveness, reconciliation, restoration, and new life.[52] Yet he also insists that those who have embraced Christ and his way of life are called to live in a similar way, for "suffering applies to his disciples."[53] Moreover, he describes the life of discipleship as an "allegiance to the suffering Christ."[54]

---

52. Bonhoeffer, *Cost of Discipleship*, 79, 80.
53. Bonhoeffer, *Cost of Discipleship*, 77.
54. Bonhoeffer, *Cost of Discipleship*, 80.

Bonhoeffer exemplified his willingness to follow the suffering Christ in his work with urban youth and his defense of the Jewish community in the face of Hitler's tyranny and oppression. He identified with marginal groups in his opposition to Hitler, and he sacrificed his career and reputation in the cause of the Confessing Church. Ultimately, his involvement with the Abwehr's attempts to overthrow Hitler cost him his life. For Bonhoeffer, suffering on behalf of others was incarnational and "redemptive," because it was a way that he could share in the suffering of Christ.

In *The Cost of Discipleship*, he traces a comprehensive theological vision for Christian suffering. He begins with our Christian initiation, noting that our incorporation into Christ involves entering a "baptismal death," where the old way of life is put aside and we are raised with Christ in newness of life. In baptism, we suffer the death of the "old self."[55]

Following our baptism, having been raised with Christ into new life, we experience a "daily dying" as we seek to do God's will rather than our own.[56] In this daily discipleship, we experience "suffering 'for him [Christ].'"[57]

Finally, we experience suffering in a "representative capacity," which reflects the way of Christ in the life of the church. Bonhoeffer describes such suffering as a "vicarious activity," where we take upon ourselves, in faith, the burdens of others so that they might find relief and healing.[58]

When the powers of this age become distorted, many people suffer—and the poor suffer always. But as Christians, we are called to join the suffering God by suffering with and for those who end up on the ash heap of life.

> *We are not able to hold out against suffering*
> *in all respects.*
> *An unexpected sorrow, though slight, goes to our heart—*
> *or a slander, or a lie people tell about us . . .*
> *How quickly and deeply any of this wounds us . . .*
> *By this we show plainly that we do not live with Christ as he lived;*
> *neither do we forsake all as Christ did;*
> *nor are we forsaken by all as Christ was.*[59]

---

55. Bonhoeffer, *Cost of Discipleship*, 207.
56. Bonhoeffer, *Cost of Discipleship*, 219.
57. Bonhoeffer, *Cost of Discipleship*, 207.
58. Bonhoeffer, *Cost of Discipleship*, 220.
59. From Hadewijch (thirteenth-century Beguine). Quoted in Ringma and Alexander, eds., *Of Martyrs, Monks, and Mystics*, 182.

6:6

A Prophetic Way of Life

Seek good and not evil,
that you may live:
and so the Lord, the God of hosts, will be with you,
just as you have said.
Hate evil and love good,
and establish justice in the gate . . .

—Amos 5:14–15

Bonhoeffer has been interpreted in many different ways and labeled as pastor, theologian, activist, radical, saint, political provocateur, and so on. Rather than using these labels, I have sought to sculpt Bonhoeffer through his own words as much as possible.

Thus far, it has become clear that Bonhoeffer was profoundly focused on Christ and strongly opposed to the idolatry of Hitler's ideology and political regime. Bonhoeffer was also deeply committed to his family and to the renewal of the church. He gave of himself through his ecumenical involvement and in training clergy for the Confessing Church. Through much struggle, he also came to believe that it was right and necessary for him to do all he could to wrest from Hitler's hands the "steering wheel" of the vehicle that the Nazis were using to destroy the most basic values of civil society.

It has also become evident that Bonhoeffer wrestled with the theological currents of his day. He wrote many important books, despite the challenging circumstances of his life, and he was committed to practicing the spiritual disciplines in his daily life. Whatever his circumstances, he engaged with others in a pastoral role—urban youth, seminarians, colleagues in the Confessing Church, and fellow prisoners.

In seeking to follow Christ and Christ's way in the world, Bonhoeffer exemplified a prophetic way of life, though he never used this language. We can identify the rough outlines of his prophetic way of life as follows.

First, he engaged Scripture and the theological movements of his day to help him discern what was distorted in the world in light of Jesus—the redeemer of the world, the icon of a new humanity, and the suffering servant of the reign of God.

Second, Bonhoeffer sought to engage the world by celebrating what was good and denouncing all that was evil. This led him to seek the renewal of the church and the renewal of life in Germany in light of the challenges he saw facing the church and the world in the twentieth century and beyond. Ultimately, this cost him his life.

As Bonhoeffer puts it, the costly way of following Jesus involves the displacement of our old existence, which "produces a new situation," where we are bound "to Jesus Christ alone."[60] He goes on to say that this way of life is marked by faith and discipleship, for only the one "who is obedient believes."[61]

Third, he argues that only those who "take upon themselves the distress and humiliation and sins of others" truly reflect Christ's love for the world.[62] As he puts it, "the incarnation is the ultimate reason why the service of God cannot be divorced from the service of man [woman]."[63]

Fourth, he reveals how the faith community embodies a prophetic way of life whenever it proclaims that Christ has made the way of salvation an open door for *all*. As Bonhoeffer puts it, "where the world oppresses," the follower of Christ "will stoop down and raise up the oppressed."[64] Though "the world exercises dominion by force,"[65] Bonhoeffer reminds us that "sovereign power belongs to God and not to the state."[66] Moreover, the faith community is called to do good "without limit or reserve."[67]

---

60. Bonhoeffer, *Cost of Discipleship*, 52.
61. Bonhoeffer, *Cost of Discipleship*, 54.
62. Bonhoeffer, *Cost of Discipleship*, 100.
63. Bonhoeffer, *Cost of Discipleship*, 117.
64. Bonhoeffer, *Cost of Discipleship*, 232.
65. Bonhoeffer, *Cost of Discipleship*, 235.
66. Bonhoeffer, *Cost of Discipleship*, 237.
67. Bonhoeffer, *Cost of Discipleship*, 236.

During Bonhoeffer's day, his prophetic way of life served as a beacon of hope in dark times. We need to recover this prophetic embodiment of Christ in our twenty-first-century church.

> *Lord, forgive my calculated efforts to serve you . . .*
> *only in the places where it is safe to do so . . .*
> *Lord, forgive me, renew me,*
> *send me out as a usable instrument*
> *that I might take seriously the meaning of your cross.*[68]

---

68. Morley, ed., *Bread of Tomorrow*, 76.

7

A Prophetic Spirituality

Introduction

IN OUR CONTEMPORARY WORLD, spirituality can mean almost anything as long as it has to do with creating some inner awareness. Within a Christian frame, spirituality involves engaging spiritual practices that reflect and sustain our life in Christ as we seek to live the way of Christ in the world to the glory of God and the blessing of our neighbor.

In a similar way, the present-day use of "prophetic" has a variety of meanings, often to do with premonitions or being able to predict something in the future. Within a Christian theological frame, the word *prophetic* is multidimensional. First, it has a receptivity component, which may be visionary—the prophet receives something from God. Second, its heart is proclamation—God has something to say to the people of God and to all humanity. Third, it has a corrective dimension—the prophet, as God's spokesperson, points out what needs to change. Fourth, it has an eschatological orientation—the prophet sculpts a picture of what God's new order will be like. Much of this multidimensional understanding of the prophetic tradition is embedded in the Old Testament.

From this starting point, we may move to the New Testament and suggest that Christ himself embodies all of the above components (and more), which makes the prophetic tradition relevant for the present-day faith community. If Christ is the great prophet, then his followers are called to exercise a prophetic ministry.

Scholars have noted that Bonhoeffer exercised a prophetic ministry,[1] which has been divided into three periods—"discipleship and community, then involvement in the struggle for peace and justice, and finally faith in a secular age."[2] These demarcations can be misleading, since Bonhoeffer was an integrated thinker, but it is clear that prophetic dimensions existed in all three periods. The prophetic nature of his ministry is particularly evident in his focus on seeking to bring about transformation in the German church and change in the sociopolitical ideology of his country.

Regarding the first phase, "discipleship and community," Bonhoeffer's writing reflects a deep concern about the need to resist Nazi ideology within the church.[3] He notes that the church needs to be much more than a place where God is "a plaything" and where people are simply "religiously inclined."[4] He writes of "the creaking and groaning of church's structures" at a time of "utter decline and breakdown."[5]

Within this setting, he calls for the renewal of the church and the activation of its mission to the world. The church is not merely part of the biblical prophetic tradition, for "it is *Christus praesens*"[6]—an icon of Christ himself. As such, it is a faith community of the resurrection, a place where "the kingdom of God itself comes to us, in our world."[7] Moreover, it is the place where the followers of Christ live their faith in "discipleship."[8]

This life of discipleship, while oriented to growing in Christ and renewing the faith community, is called to carry a deep concern about the world. In prayer and service, the faith community binds itself "to the Earth, to misery, to hunger, to death," and lives in the "most profound solidarity with the world."[9]

This brings us to Bonhoeffer's second phase, the "struggle for peace and justice."[10] In his writings on this theme, he makes it clear that Christ "is the center and strength of the Bible, of the church, and of theology, but also

---

1. Haynes, *Bonhoeffer Phenomenon*, 37–63.
2. de Gruchy, ed., *Cambridge Companion to Dietrich Bonhoeffer*, 103.
3. de Gruchy, ed., *Cambridge Companion to Dietrich Bonhoeffer*, 103.
4. Bonhoeffer, *Works*, vol. 12, *Berlin 1932–1933*, 263.
5. Bonhoeffer, *Works*, vol. 12, 477, 459.
6. Bonhoeffer, *Works*, vol. 12, 83.
7. Bonhoeffer, *Works*, vol. 12, 291.
8. Bonhoeffer, *Works*, vol. 12, 259.
9. Bonhoeffer, *Works*, vol. 12, 289.
10. de Gruchy, ed., *Cambridge Companion to Dietrich Bonhoeffer*, 103.

A Prophetic Spirituality

of humanity, of reason, of justice, and of culture."[11] In engaging the world and all of life, Bonhoeffer suggests that the Christian task is not to spread general Christian values into society, but rather to live as a servant of the kingdom of God. As such, the church "gives witness to the miracle of God," bearing witness to the good news that *all* are included in Christ's redemption and *all* dimensions of life will be renewed.[12] Thus the faith community is called to "question the state" and "protect the state from itself."[13]

In the third phase of Bonhoeffer's ministry, "faith in a secular age,"[14] he wrestles with the problem of secularity. In these writings, he notes how humanity has become central, without the "'working hypothesis' called 'God.'"[15] He goes on to explain that in a "world that has come of age," the proclamation of the church regarding Christ must retain "elements of genuine prophecy"—such as the claim to truth and mercy.[16] Moreover, he insists that the "full content" of the New Testament must be proclaimed and lived.[17] Bonhoeffer also warns that secularity should not be understood on its own terms, "but on the basis of the gospel, and in the light of Christ."[18]

For Bonhoeffer, the prophetic witness of those who follow Christ is not some special task given to a few. Rather, it is intrinsic to being a Christian, for all Christians are called to proclaim to the world through word and deed that Christ is the great prophet and suffering servant, who dwells within us by the Spirit.

Bonhoeffer is careful to point out that our redemption in Christ does not simply redeem us *from* "cares, distress, fears, and . . . from sin and death," but beckons us to participate *in* and *with* Christ so that we "drink the earthly cup to the dregs."[19] In this way, we proclaim that "the crucified and risen Christ" is with us and that we are "with Christ."[20]

---

11. Bonhoeffer, *Ethics*, 58.
12. Bonhoeffer, *Works*, vol. 12, *Berlin 1932–1933*, 293.
13. Bonhoeffer, *Works*, vol. 12, 365, 366.
14. de Gruchy, ed., *Cambridge Companion to Dietrich Bonhoeffer*, 103.
15. Bonhoeffer, *Letters and Papers*, 325.
16. Bonhoeffer, *Letters and Papers*, 327, 328.
17. Bonhoeffer, *Letters and Papers*, 329.
18. Bonhoeffer, *Letters and Papers*, 329.
19. Bonhoeffer, *Letters and Papers*, 336.
20. Bonhoeffer, *Letters and Papers*, 337.

7:1

The Call of God

*"Before I formed you in the womb I knew you,
and before you were born I consecrated you;
I appointed you a prophet to the nations."*

—Jeremiah 1:5

At a very young age, Bonhoeffer declared to his family that he wanted to become a theologian and wanted to change the church for the better. Later in life, after he had completed his theological studies and come to a living faith in Christ and the gospel, this initial desire became a reality. Yet this reality was most likely well beyond his wildest imaginings!

Even in Bonhoeffer's earliest writings, he had a growing sense of what it meant to be a disciple of Christ. He writes that discipleship involves an "allegiance to the suffering Christ."[21] And he explains that when we are bound "to Jesus Christ alone," we live a life of "displacement from the old existence."[22] Moreover, rather than following a set program for life, the disciple of Christ is called to a "life of absolute insecurity."[23]

Bonhoeffer insists that such a life must be marked by obedience to the gospel and the leading of the Spirit, for "*only* [the one] who believes is obedient, and *only* [the one] who is obedient believes."[24] He also emphasizes the role of the Spirit, for "the entire fullness of the Holy Spirit wants to unfold and ripen" in us, and therefore we should give the Spirit "full space within us."[25]

In seeking to follow Christ, Bonhoeffer lived this dynamic reality of Word and Spirit. Time and again, he "heard" the call of God to proclaim,

---

21. Bonhoeffer, *Cost of Discipleship*, 80.
22. Bonhoeffer, *Cost of Discipleship*, 52–53.
23. Bonhoeffer, *Cost of Discipleship*, 49.
24. Bonhoeffer, *Cost of Discipleship*, 54 (emphasis in original).
25. Bonhoeffer, *Works*, vol. 16, *Conspiracy and Imprisonment 1940–1945*, 628.

A Prophetic Spirituality

teach, pray, and act. First, he heard the call to criticize Hitler's concept of leadership. Second, he heard the call to condemn and resist Hitler's mandate to exclude Jewish Christians from leadership roles in the church. Third, he heard the call to return to Germany from his involvement with a German congregation in London. Fourth, he heard the call to help create the Confessing Church. Fifth, he heard the call to return to Germany from the safety of the United States just as World War II was about to darken Europe and the rest of the world. Sixth, he heard the call to join the Abwehr in its resistance to Hitler.

Bonhoeffer's entire life was marked by obedient following. Again and again, he was called—and again and again, he acted.

This witness is very important for us in the twenty-first century, for our contemporary consumer Christianity, particularly in the West, needs a major reorientation. We, who already have so much, tend to focus on God's *gifts* to us rather than how God is *calling* us. We have made the blessings of Christ a mere add-on to the rest of our lives. Christ has become the convenient comforter, who guarantees that we will be blessed in the afterlife.

Though Bonhoeffer received great comfort from Christ, and he believed in the fullness of life in God's final future, he also believed that Christ is Lord of the church and "the center of human existence, of history, and of nature."[26] Because Christ is Lord over all, Bonhoeffer insists that Christians are called to participate in every dimension of life—both the "sacred" and the "secular."

For Bonhoeffer, Christian existence is not simply about what we believe, but rather being called again and again by the gospel and the Spirit to live as the suffering servant of Christ in the world in order to seek its full healing and restoration.

May we hear this call today and gladly follow Christ into our wounded world.

> *The . . . thing that pertains to a good person*
> *is that he or she must in all things*
> *be obedient to God,*
> *and to holy church,*
> *and to proper convictions.*
> *And to each of these three there must be equal obedience:*
> *so shall the person live without care and doubt,*
> *and shall ever abide without inward approach in all his or her deeds.*[27]

26. Bonhoeffer, *Christ the Center*, 60.

27. From Jan van Ruysbroeck (1293–1381). Quoted in Ringma and Alexander, *Of Martyrs, Monks, and Mystics*, 126.

7:2

The Shaping of Life

Let the word of Christ dwell in you richly; teach and admonish one another in all wisdom; and with gratitude in your hearts sing psalms, hymns, and spiritual songs to God. And whatever you do, in word or deed, do everything in the name of the Lord Jesus, giving thanks to the Father through him.

—COLOSSIANS 3:16–17

A prophetic spirituality is not so much a special gift as it is a way of life that can be shaped by social, spiritual, and situational factors, among others.

Those who have a prophetic orientation are, first of all, *oriented towards God*. Second, they are *inwardly aware*. Third, they are able to *read the signs of the times*.

In living this trilectic (three-dimensional) existence, the prophet must first know God and listen to God. Second, the prophet must be inwardly attuned to the Spirit of God and therefore receptive and compliant to the Spirit's leading. Third, the prophet must be aware of the issues and concerns of the world, specifically regarding his or her sociocultural context. While a prophet's words may have wider implications, his or her words are usually addressed to specific situations.

We see this prophetic trilectic ever so clearly in the life and ministry of Dietrich Bonhoeffer. Bonhoeffer's life was profoundly shaped by the goodness and values of his family. His theological formation helped him to listen attentively to Scripture and the theological tradition of the church. This background helped him develop a vision of the church as a second "incarnation" of Christ that is called to engage the world in prophetic witness and through vicarious suffering.

In opposing the politics of Hitler and seeking to reform the German church in light of its captivity to Nazi ideology, Bonhoeffer committed to

A Prophetic Spirituality

work with others to form the Confessing Church. Through these involvements, he engaged the challenges of his time through prophetic action.

It is important to note that prophetic spirituality is not about harping on things that are bad in society, nor is it a form of wishful thinking about how things could be better. Moreover, prophetic spirituality is not merely a ministry of prayer for evil to be overcome and good to flourish (though prayer, which Bonhoeffer describes as "the supreme instance of the hidden character of the Christian life," is essential).[28] Rather, prophetic spirituality is about being "pregnant" with the holy and with God's passion for the renewal of the church and the restoration of society.

Jesus makes it clear that we cannot live the Christian life unless we seek to love God and love neighbor. Thus God's passion for goodness, truth, well-being, and shalom cannot be reserved for one segment of life, but is intended for *all* of life—spirituality, family, community, economics, the arts, and politics.

In emphasizing this point, Bonhoeffer writes, "Just as in Christ the reality of God entered into the reality of the world, so, too, is that which is Christian is to be found only *in* that which is of the world, the 'supernatural' only *in* the natural, the holy *in* the profane."[29] He notes that we cannot think of "the spiritual sphere" as "an end in itself," nor the secular sphere as independent and self-existent, because "the gospel . . . is addressed to the whole world."[30]

Prophetic spirituality can be described as *agonistic*, for it continually agonizes about what *is* and what *could be*. It wrestles with the waywardness of the church while also challenging the world. It also wrestles with God, particularly God's seeming slowness in bringing about change and renewal. Moreover, prophetic spirituality can be described as *identificational*, for it identifies itself with Christ and also with the suffering world.

In conclusion, Bonhoeffer insists that Christians "must have some share in Christ's large-heartedness" and act "with responsibility and in freedom" to express the "redeeming love of Christ for all who suffer."[31]

In some parts of the world people face a total system of death,
of monstrous false gods,
of exploitative economic systems, of violence,

---

28. Bonhoeffer, *Cost of Discipleship*, 146.
29. Bonhoeffer, *Ethics*, 196 (emphasis in original).
30. Bonhoeffer, *Ethics*, 196, 197.
31. Bonhoeffer, *Letters and Papers from Prison*, 14.

of the disintegration of the fundamental bonds of human society,
of the destruction of human life . . .
We are called to exercise our mission in this context of human struggle,
and challenged to keep the earth alive
and to promote human dignity . . .
since the living God is . . . the protector of the cause of the widow,
the orphan, the poor and the stranger.[32]

---

32. Scherer and Bevans, eds., "Mission in Christ's Way," in *New Directions*, 74.

7:3

Into the Struggle

"Come, let us return to the Lord;
for it is he who has torn us, and he will heal us;
he has struck down, and he will bind us up."

—Hosea 6:1

While some people pray that things in our society will change, and others creatively work for change, few are willing to confront those who misuse their positions and power in order to call them to accountability and justice.

When we confront the God-ordained powers of social governance that have become distorted, we begin to realize how small we are before the state's ideology, laws, propaganda, and institutions of compliance and force. While most hope that these powers will be used for good, many experience a nightmare when they go astray.

Bonhoeffer lived during a time when "normal" life had been turned upside down. In his personal writings, he laments how "chaos is at the door" and "the air we breathe is... polluted by mistrust."[33] He describes the world around him as having been "torn into fragments by events."[34]

Amidst these chaotic circumstances, Bonhoeffer believed that Christians were called to resist the powers with courage and to work towards change and renewal. He understood that renewal needed to begin in the church, and so he helped to form the Confessing Church, which he hoped would help change the social and political order of his day.

Yet in his writing, he acknowledges the fragility of resistance and creative engagement. In his poems, he speaks of "trembling with anger at

---

33. Bonhoeffer, *Letters and Papers*, 12, 11.
34. Bonhoeffer, *Letters and Papers*, 200.

despotism" while also confessing that he feels like a "woebegone weakling."[35] In the same line, he speaks of being "defiant" and "despondent."[36]

Though Bonhoeffer insists that God *waits* for "our prayers and responsible actions,"[37] he makes it clear that prophetic resistance is not about seeking to be "dare-devils," but rather being sustained in the "courage that comes from the grace of God."[38]

It is important to note that prophetic spirituality has nothing to do with ironclad certainties, for it is birthed in the contested space of discernment and struggle, where we are plagued with questions and uncertainty. *Do I really understand what is happening in our society when so many seem to think that everything is just fine? Have I really "heard" the voice of God? Are my actions of proclamation and resistance consistent with my beliefs? Can I be certain that there will be good outcomes?*

Bonhoeffer felt called to create a "social order based on equality," and he believed that Christians should respond to people "in the light of what they suffer."[39] He made it clear that neither "resignation" nor "pious escapism" were answers to the troubles of his time.[40] Instead, he called Christians to respond with "sympathy and action" as a way of sharing in Christ's "large-heartedness."[41]

Christ, the true prophet, welcomed the marginalized poor and engaged them through his ministry of healing and also by confronting those in power who were corrupting human well-being. Moreover, Christ created a movement of shalom that reflected something of God's reign on earth as it is in heaven.

> *The Church of Jesus Christ is commissioned to disciple the nations,*
> *so that others may know that the kingdom of God*
> *has already drawn near....*
> *Mission that is conscious of the kingdom will be concerned*
> *with liberation, not oppression;*
> *justice, not exploitation;*
> *fullness, not deprivation;*

---

35. Bonhoeffer, *Letters and Papers*, 348.
36. Bonhoeffer, *Letters and Papers*, 351.
37. Bonhoeffer, *Letters and Papers*, 11.
38. Bonhoeffer, *Letters and Papers*, 156.
39. Bonhoeffer, *Letters and Papers*, 13, 10.
40. Bonhoeffer, *Letters and Papers*, 15.
41. Bonhoeffer, *Letters and Papers*, 15, 14.

freedom, not slavery;
health, not disease;
life, not death.[42]

---

42. Scherer and Bevans, eds., "Your Kingdom Come," in *New Directions,* 29.

7:4

Confronting the Powers

He is the image of the invisible God, the firstborn of all creation; for in him all things in heaven and earth were created, things visible and invisible, whether thrones or dominions or rulers or powers—all things have been created through him and for him.

—COLOSSIANS 1:15–16

Throughout the Gospels, we can see Christ as a friend of the poor, outcast, and marginalized. We can also see him as someone who honored women and children in a society of hierarchy. And we can see him as a forgiving savior and healer. But there is much more about Christ that needs to be celebrated!

Bonhoeffer makes it clear that Christ is far more than the Lord of our inner piety, the gateway to heaven, or the Lord of the church, for he argues that Christ is the "center of human existence, of history, and of nature."[43] As the Lord of human existence, Christ seeks to redeem each of us as "a person before God."[44] As the Lord of history, Christ destroys all "corrupt messianic promises."[45] And as the Lord of nature, Christ redeems all of "enslaved nature . . . in hope."[46]

In Bonhoeffer's grand articulation of the person and work of Christ, he celebrates Christ's lordship over all the domains of life and all the powers. He proclaims that in Christ, there is the "end of the old world," since Christ is "for the whole of human existence."[47]

Bonhoeffer's vision of Christ's lordship also challenges the autonomy and power of the state. While other powers may have influence over our

---

43. Bonhoeffer, *Christ the Center*, 60.
44. Bonhoeffer, *Christ the Center*, 61.
45. Bonhoeffer, *Christ the Center*, 62.
46. Bonhoeffer, *Christ the Center*, 65.
47. Bonhoeffer, *Christ the Center*, 65.

A Prophetic Spirituality

lives, only the state lays claim to ultimate earthly power in terms of sovereignty, legislative power, social control, and various forms of coercion.

Yet Bonhoeffer ascribes a limiting dimension to the power of the state by arguing that we "must see the state in the light of Christ."[48] Practically, this means that the state can *never* be the final word for the Christian, for God must be obeyed, first and foremost.

Bonhoeffer claims that because of God's entry in Christ into history, "the order of the state has been finally broken through and dissolved."[49] This certainly does not mean that Bonhoeffer rejects the role of the state, but he does reject its claim to *ultimate* power. Thus he asserts that in the light of Christ, the state can be "affirmed and fulfilled,"[50] but its power is limited under God's ultimate lordship.

This has been practically demonstrated again and again in the long march of the church through history. Early Christians in the Roman Empire refused to acknowledge the lordship of Caesar. In the Middle Ages, Christian sectarian movements—the Waldensians and the Albigenses, among others—refused to submit to the power of the Holy Roman Empire. In the modern world, Christians refused to obey the claims of the state regarding the chattel nature of slavery and helped to facilitate the escape of slaves from oppressive conditions. And during Bonhoeffer's time, he and others refused to obey Hitler's initial marginalization of Jewish people, which subsequently led to the mistreatment and elimination of millions of Jews.

Christians are called to live as a conservative force in the world, but our purpose is to conserve what is good, not to condone evil. We are called to make peace, work for justice, and engage the tasks of reconciliation and healing, but we are also called to resist the distorted powers of our time and to raise our voices in prophetic witness.

> *Jesus intends his followers neither to withdraw from the world*
> *in order to preserve their holiness,*
> *nor to lose their holiness by conforming to the world,*
> *but simultaneously to permeate the world*
> *and retain their kingdom distinctives.*[51]

---

48. Bonhoeffer, *Christ the Center*, 64.
49. Bonhoeffer, *Christ the Center*, 63.
50. Bonhoeffer, *Christ the Center*, 63.
51. Stott, ed., "The Grand Rapids Report on Evangelism and Social Responsibility," in *Making Christ Known*, 189–90.

7:5

A New Vision

Is this not the fast that I choose:
to loose the bonds of injustice,
to undo the thongs of the yoke,
to let the oppressed go free,
and to break every yoke?

—Isaiah 58:6

The faith community lives in the light of a number of biblical mandates, which we are called to embrace, live by, and seek to incarnate in the world.

First, the *creation mandate* calls us to be concerned with caring for the earth and shaping both the environment and the social order. This is one of the most general mandates in Scripture.

Second, the *redemptive mandate* calls us to embrace God's salvation and restoration. Since all fall far short of who we should be in fulfilling the purposes of God, this mandate calls us to a full recovery of God's renewing purposes for the world.

Third, the *relational mandate* calls us to love God and also to love the neighbor. This mandate calls us to form community *in* Christ and to be community *for* the world.

Fourth, the *missional mandate* calls the faith community to bear witness to the good news in Christ and to serve the world in light of God's purposes of forgiveness, healing, peacemaking, and justice.

Fifth, the *eschatological mandate* calls us to live in the here and the now in the light of God's final future. Simply put, we are called to live in the present while straining toward what God will *yet* do. Marked by the inbreaking of the presence and reign of God in Christ through the Spirit, we are called to pray and to work so that God's kingdom will more fully come into our lives and our world. And if the dominant values of our society do not reflect God's purposes for humanity, this mandate calls us to resist what is death-dealing in our culture and to live as a prophetic witness of God's renewal.

Bonhoeffer makes this point more generally when he explains that "the church-community recognizes itself as an instrument of God's will, and accordingly organizes itself in active obedience."[52] Bonhoeffer locates the genesis of our obedience in serving God's purposes in "inspired Scripture."[53] Furthermore, he maintains that such obedience is the "proper and *singular* principle of theology."[54]

He also argues that when we appropriate Scripture through meditative practices, scholarly engagement, or proclamation, it "confronts us, seizes us, takes us captive."[55] Such language conveys that for Bonhoeffer, the biblical narratives provide us with both the inspiration for and shape of our engagement in society.

At the same time, Bonhoeffer acknowledges that this challenging and directive word of Christ is "effectively brought to the heart of the hearers by the Spirit."[56] Because the Spirit inspires and directs us in our witness and service, Bonhoeffer challenges us to live in such a way as to give "full space" to the Spirit "for the sake of God [and] for the sake of others."[57]

Yet living a life of obedience to God that is devoted to seeing God's purposes unfold in our world is not the task of a solo Christian. Rather, it is the task of the whole faith community, which is called to proclaim that *all* are provided for in Christ while both resisting the worldliness of the world and living in anticipation of God's final future.

> *We ought simply to follow where God leads,*
> *that is, to do what we are most inclined to do,*
> *to go where we are repeatedly admonished to go—*
> *to where we feel most drawn.*
> *If we do that,*
> *God gives us his greatest in our least*
> *and never fails.*[58]

52. Bonhoeffer, *Works*, vol. 1, *Sanctorum Communio*, 188.
53. Bonhoeffer, *Works*, vol. 9, *Young Bonhoeffer, 1918–1927*, 302.
54. Bonhoeffer, *Works*, vol. 9, 302 (emphasis in original).
55. Bonhoeffer, *Works*, vol. 13, *London 1933–1935*, 350.
56. Bonhoeffer, *Works*, vol. 1, *Sanctorum Communio*, 158.
57. Bonhoeffer, *Works*, vol. 16, *Conspiracy and Imprisonment 1940–1945*, 628.
58. From Meister Eckhart (c. 1260–1327). Quoted in Ringma and Alexander, eds., *Of Martyrs, Monks, and Mystics*, 114.

7:6

Vicarious Suffering

Remember Jesus Christ, raised from the dead, a descendent of David—that is my gospel, for which I suffer hardship, even to the point of being chained like a criminal. But the word of God is not chained.

—2 Timothy 2:8–9

In the long journey of the church through history, it has been both a persecuted minority and a powerful institution. To a significant degree, the church has always found itself in living in and between these polarities. In certain societies, the church is a marginalized group. In other settings, it seeks to gain political credibility and have a greater influence.

Bonhoeffer lived during a time when the church in Germany was seeking political power through its compliance with Nazi ideology. As a consequence, Bonhoeffer was compelled to assert that "we must disobey a heretical church regime for the sake of Christ even if it is appointed by the state."[59] He also wrestled with the role of the church in society in light of the relationship between power and suffering.

His answer to this challenging issue was christological. He writes that Christ, in his death and resurrection, is the *"vicarious representative"* for all of humanity, and therefore Christ demonstrates that redemptive suffering is the way to freedom and healing.[60] Bonhoeffer elaborates by explaining that Christ "bears the whole burden of man's [woman's] separation from God" through his "redemptive efficacy."[61] The faith community, which is born to new life in Christ and called to Christlikeness, must therefore live in the world in a similar way.

---

59. Bonhoeffer, *Works*, vol. 15, *Theological Education Underground 1937–1940*, 433.
60. Bonhoeffer, *Works*, vol. 1, *Sanctorum Communio*, 155 (emphasis in original).
61. Bonhoeffer, *Cost of Discipleship*, 81, 82.

A Prophetic Spirituality

Bonhoeffer makes it clear that the church is called to live in "the way of Christ."[62] Moreover, he says that "it is with this humiliated [Christ] that the Church goes its own way of humiliation."[63] The church can live out this challenging call to follow "the way of Christ" and "its own way of humiliation" by not seeking political privileges, refusing to align itself with those in power, challenging those who misuse power, taking the side of the oppressed, and being willing to suffer the consequences of living this particular way.[64] But most fundamentally, the faith community is called to become more fully converted and oriented to the *way* of Christ.

Bonhoeffer insists that true Christian discipleship involves "allegiance to the suffering Christ."[65] He explains that the follower of Christ is to live a "baptismal death which is the fountain of grace" and that this "baptized life . . . [is] a constant renewal of . . . faith in the death of Christ."[66]

Bonhoeffer describes Christ in seemingly contradictory ways, speaking of his "exaltation and humiliation"[67] while also insisting that "incarnate one is the glorified God."[68] Yet in these paradoxical descriptions, Bonhoeffer identifies Christ as one who does not move towards greater power, but towards greater servanthood and suffering on behalf of others. Thus in following Christ, the faith community is called *not* to seek political power or social and cultural conformity, but rather to be willing to give *away* power for the sake and well-being of the other.

Such a kenotic spirituality will call us to walk a most painful and cruciform path as we seek to live the upside-down ways of the kingdom of God within our refractory world.

As Bonhoeffer puts it, "we have seen the exalted one, only as the crucified; the sinless one, only as the guilt-laden; the risen one, only as the humiliated."[69] And as followers of this Christ, we are called to live in the power of that vision.

Had Jesus merely said that his mission was to set people free
from sin and all forms of oppression,

---

62. Bonhoeffer, *Christ the Center*, 113.
63. Bonhoeffer, *Christ the Center*, 113.
64. Bonhoeffer, *Christ the Center*, 113.
65. Bonhoeffer, *Cost of Discipleship*, 80.
66. Bonhoeffer, *Cost of Discipleship*, 207, 210.
67. Bonhoeffer, *Christ the Center*, 57.
68. Bonhoeffer, *Christ the Center*, 105.
69. Bonhoeffer, *Christ the Center*, 112.

his words would have fallen on deaf ears . . .
He not only talked of freeing the poor and oppressed but, undeterred by criticism,
actually welcomed the poor and sinners to share at his table.
Like Jesus, we must be able to accompany others in their suffering
and be willing to suffer with them.[70]

---

70. Scherer and Bevans, eds., "To the Ends of the Earth," in *New Directions*, 141.

8

Engaging Society

Introduction

BECAUSE WE LIVE IN society and are shaped by its life and values, we are all products of our particular time and place. While there is much we can be grateful for in many societies, poverty, oppression, and corruption are major concerns in other societies.

Moreover, those who hold power in most contexts are seeking to shape the social world according to their own vision and priorities, doing their very best to catechize the rest of society accordingly. To put this more clearly, no society is neutral, and no society is based on true equality. Thus there are always the "haves" and the "have-nots."

Even more disconcerting, those in power—while claiming to serve all—are often only serving their own interests. So from political leaders, we repeatedly hear the mantra that whatever they are doing is in "the national interest." Or, in the world of business, leaders justify their actions by saying that they are "serving shareholders." But all too often, such decisions are self-serving and do not benefit the common good.

In light of these and other factors, it is not surprising that many people feel discouraged and pessimistic about those in power and tend to distrust the major institutions in society.

This raises a question about how Christians are called to live amidst such circumstances—and more specifically, what we can learn from Bonhoeffer. For while our world is different from Bonhoeffer's, it is still full of many similar challenges. And even though the church can engage society in many ways, it can't bring heaven to earth, nor can it right every wrong, and it should not seek to bring about a christological utopia.

Yet the faith community can seek to live God's restorative vision with fidelity through prayer, witness, winsome persuasion, and loving service while trusting the sovereign and mysterious workings of God through the Spirit to effect change. In other words, the church can never *possess* God, but it can live as God's *possession*.

Bonhoeffer believed that the faith community must first be grounded in Christ through the Spirit and then seek to live a life of discipleship while engaging society in prophetic and transformational ways. He also believed that following this life of discipleship in Christ would come at great personal cost.

Throughout his writing, he stresses that the church has a divine mandate to tell the world that something magnificent has taken place for the well-being of all—namely, that in Christ's death and resurrection, there is an abundant provision available for the redemption and renewal of the whole world. He also insists that the church is called to proclaim this wonderful news by *living* it in exemplary ways.

At the same time, the church is called to pray for and to challenge the world when the powers of society cease to serve the common good and the quest for peace and justice. This places the church in the crosshairs between the state and other forms of institutional power.

Bonhoeffer had no illusion that the church in his time was doing this well, for he saw the church deteriorate in Germany as it was seduced by Nazi ideology. Thus Bonhoeffer was faced with a double task—to seek the renewal of the church and to live as a liberating voice and force in the world.

8:1

God's Heart for the World

For in him all the fullness of God was pleased to dwell, and through him God was pleased to reconcile to himself all things, whether on earth or in heaven, by making peace through the blood of his cross.

—COLOSSIANS 1:19–20

God's heart for the world is perpetually "wounded," as God is always seeking to bring home the wandering daughters and sons who are lost, confused, and broken. Scripture repeatedly tells this story of God's wounded heart for the wounded world and God's ongoing longing to bring about healing and restoration for all.

Because God's heart is wounded, God's action in the world is driven by compassionate love for all of wayward humanity, and so God has made a way to bring *all* home through Christ's redemptive suffering.

The biblical narratives tell the story of a God who is both wholly *other* and also wholly *concerned*. Again and again, God strains towards a wayward humanity, which is often indifferent and resistant to God's goodness and favor.

Of course, some read Scripture very differently, seeing God as an authoritarian who makes endless demands. Others see God as the great and severe spoiler who only brings us joy.

Even though God does issue commands, God also beckons, persuades, and woos humans to become open and receptive to all the ways that God is seeking to bless and heal the world. While this may surprise us, God's intention is not to control us, but to give us joyful freedom as we live in God's grace and goodness. God is always seeking to make us better so that we can more fully become the people we need to be in the world.

God's heart for the world is wider than the ocean, and God has a grand vision and a great purpose for each of our lives and for the whole world.

This includes forgiveness and healing for all as well as the upliftment of the poor, the creation of institutions that serve the common good, the building of community, and the healing of our wounded planet. It also includes hope for the world to come and the creation of new heavens and a new earth in God's final future. The scope of this story is far greater than we can ever describe or imagine!

Bonhoeffer celebrates his joy that through Christ's death and resurrection, "God will make everything new again."[1] And he is adamant that "God will cause grace and compassion to radiate over the dark guilt of our century and the human race."[2]

He stresses that all "Christians ought to do what is good"[3] in every domain of life—family, church, the marketplace, the arts, and politics. But he also insists that Christians must "die to the world in the midst of their worldly calling."[4] In other words, Christians are called to sing God's song and work in the world in ways that please God while also seeking to follow God's purposes for humanity and for the whole world.

Because God's heart for the world is to make *all* things new, this expansive and inclusive vision must shape our hearts, too. We are all called to carry out the works of God amidst our time in God's way, which is always the way of love. As followers of Christ, God's love permeates our very being, for as Bonhoeffer notes, "the love of God [is] given to our hearts by the Holy Spirit."[5]

Though we may falter and fail at times, God's faithfulness will restore us, leading us from "death to life," as Bonhoeffer puts it.[6] Moreover, he insists that "the new humanity which, in hope, overcomes the history of sin and death"[7] is sure and secure in the faithfulness of the God, the Alpha and Omega.

Participating actively in God's mission through the power of the Holy Spirit means that the church prays and acts for the salvation and life of the entire creation . . . the church invokes God to send his Spirit upon all

---

1. Bonhoeffer, *Works*, vol. 10, *Barcelona, Berlin, New York 1928–1931*, 358.
2. Bonhoeffer, *Works*, vol. 10, 359.
3. Bonhoeffer, *Works*, vol. 4, *Discipleship*, 244.
4. Bonhoeffer, *Works*, vol. 4, 245.
5. Bonhoeffer, *Works*, vol. 1, *Sanctorum Communio*, 168.
6. Bonhoeffer, *Works*, vol. 10, *Barcelona, Berlin, New York 1928–1931*, 489.
7. Bonhoeffer, *Works*, vol. 1, *Sanctorum Communio*, 63.

Engaging Society

*for the sanctification and unity in Christ of the faithful,
as well as to sustain, redeem, and sanctify
the whole created world.*[8]

---

8. Scherer and Bevans, eds., "Final Report of the Commission on World Mission and Evangelism Orthodox Advisory Group," in *New Directions*, 244.

8:2

The Gift of Discernment

I have given you as a covenant to the people,
a light to the nations,
to open the eyes that are blind,
to bring out the prisoners from the dungeon,
from the prison those who sit in darkness.

—Isaiah 42:6–7

Discernment is both a gift and a process. Through Word and Spirit, God gives us the *gift* of wisdom. When we wrestle with who God wants us to be and what God wants us to do amidst the realities of our daily life, we engage the *process* of discernment. Yet none of this is easy and straightforward, for discernment involves prayer, waiting, wrestling, and committing to act in certain ways as we seek to respond faithfully to the issues and needs of our community and world. Because discernment is a multidirectional process, it is important to identify some of its core features.

First, we must discern who God wants us to be. Most fundamentally, we are called to live as a people who praise God and are sustained by the community of faith so that we can be a blessing to others and to our world.

Second, we must discern what we are called to do, a process that is both complex and situational. As we seek to fulfill the purposes of God for our world, we will be called to engage a wide range of activities—including participating in God's redemption, creation care, the work of shalom, and the quest for justice. Yet we can only act in the world in specific and situational ways.

Bonhoeffer can help us, for he sought to live out the biblical and theological vision of God's purposes for the world in his time. Shaped by the conviction that "in Christ the reality of God entered into the reality of world," he insisted that the task of the faith community was to bear witness to "the world . . . [as those] loved by God and reconciled with Him."⁹ Our witness to God's love includes the work of proclamation, reconciliation, peacemaking, and justice.

Bonhoeffer discerned the specific ways that he was called to live out God's vision of love for the world by listening to the challenge from others, reading Scripture, and working with others in the faith community. In *Letters and Papers from Prison*, he makes it clear that much of his writings are reflections on "concrete experience" based on his conviction that he was "called to obedient and responsible action in faith in exclusive allegiance to God."[10]

As a Christian activist, Bonhoeffer was also a person of prayer, and he believed that God would faithfully guide him in who he needed to be and what he needed to do. While he lived during a time of great turmoil, where "the air we breathe is . . . polluted by mistrust,"[11] he believed that he was called to find ways to cooperate with others in the task of resistance and prophetic witness. As he writes, God is waiting for our "prayers and responsible actions," and so we need to learn to trust and "put our very lives into the hands of others."[12]

From these reflections, we may say that discernment involves the joy of prayer. Yet our prayer in this context is not about asking for *things*, but rather seeking "to *become* so quiet that we *perceive* God's word to us."[13]

Discernment can also come to us through conversation with others, for Bonhoeffer speaks of the need for "fresh discourse, . . . saying controversial things," and wrestling with the "important issues of life."[14]

Bonhoeffer teaches us that our engagement with the world must be both thoughtful and prayerful as we seek to hear God's heart for the world and discern how we can best respond through "sincere prayer and responsible actions."[15]

Christians must always be aware of the influence of the Holy Spirit and be prepared to follow wherever

---

9. Bonhoeffer, *Ethics*, 196, 200.

10. Bonhoeffer, *Letters and Papers from Prison*, 3, 5.

11. Bonhoeffer, *Letters and Papers*, 11.

12. Bonhoeffer, *Letters and Papers*, 11, 12.

13. Bonhoeffer, *Works*, vol. 10, *Barcelona, Berlin, New York 1928–1931*, 577 (emphasis in original).

14. Bonhoeffer, *Works*, vol. 8, *Letters and Papers from Prison*, 498.

15. Bonhoeffer, *Works*, vol. 8, 46.

in God's providence and design the Spirit is leading them....
It belongs to the Spirit to inspire both the Church's
proclamation and the obedience of faith.[16]

---

16. "Dialogue and Proclamation," *Pontifical Council for Interreligious Dialogue, section 84.* Accessed online, https://www.vatican.va/roman_curia/pontifical_councils/interelg/documents/rc_pc_interelg_doc_19051991_dialogue-and-proclamatio_en.html.

8:3

Radical Identification

"If I am not doing the works of the Father, then do not believe in me. But if I do them, even though you do not believe me, believe the works, so that you may know and understand that the Father is in me and I am in the Father."

—John 10:37–38

Christian spirituality is three-dimensional. Most fundamentally, it is oriented towards God; second, it is concerned with personal growth; third, it is oriented towards the neighbor, the other, and the stranger.

Our identity in Christ is God's transformational and empowering gift, which renews us and gives us a new center, a new orientation, and a new way of living our life. No domain of life is outside of God's salvation, concern, and lordship.

Jesus is our model in this way of life, for his most fundamental orientation was to be *in* the Father, to please the Father, and do the works of the Father. Out of this radical orientation towards God, Jesus sought to fulfill God's purposes in redeeming the world.

When we speak of radical identification, we may first think of the call to identify with the poor, marginalized, and oppressed. And while we need to hear this call, this is not our starting point, for we must begin with who God is and what God has already done in Christ through the Spirit.

Our most radical identity is that we are joined with Christ and his redemptive purposes for the world. As we identify with Christ and his purposes, we will seek to live among and serve the faith community in its life together. This sacramental community will then call us to live as a second "incarnation" of Christ as we seek to listen to, respond to, and embody the gospel in the world in our time.

As we live the Beatitudes as a faith community, we will be drawn into the work of peace, reconciliation, healing, and restoration. Out of our radical identification with Christ, we can serve others and the world in challenging ways as we make costly sacrifices so that others may be blessed, including the poor and oppressed.

These themes reverberate throughout Bonhoeffer's writings. He speaks of the grace of Christ expressing itself in a life of discipleship as we seek to obey Christ's claim on our life. He insists that "faith is only real when there is obedience."[17] Thus we must be willing to make sacrifices and to suffer in "allegiance to the suffering Christ."[18]

Yet this life of discipleship is not a solo journey, for Bonhoeffer insists that it must be expressed within the "disciple community" as a "fellowship of the beatitudes" and in solidarity with "the Crucified."[19] Grounded in Christ and living for Christ, the faith community seeks to be a *"vicarious representative"* of Christ.[20]

Bonhoeffer explains that this community of faith, while "belonging wholly to Christ," also lives the dialectic of "standing at the same time wholly in the world."[21] Its task in the world is to proclaim and embody through its life together that "the world . . . [is] loved by God and reconciled with him."[22]

In following the way of Christ, the faith community must question, resist, and overcome everything in the world that does not resonate with God's great beneficence. Through witness and service, all who follow Christ are called to reject every form of coercion and to share the "same mind" that was in Christ Jesus by seeking to empty ourselves, taking "the form of a slave," and becoming "obedient to the point of death" (Phil 2:7–8).

> *But the love which impels the Church to communicate to all people*
> *a sharing in the grace of divine life . . .*
> *causes her . . . to pursue people's true temporal good . . . [and]*
> *an integral liberation from everything that hinders the development of individuals.*
> *The Church desires the good of man [woman] in all his [hers] dimensions,*
> *first of all, as a member of the city of God, and then as a member of the earthly city.*[23]

---

17. Bonhoeffer, *Cost of Discipleship*, 54.
18. Bonhoeffer, *Cost of Discipleship*, 80.
19. Bonhoeffer, *Cost of Discipleship*, 106, 103.
20. Bonhoeffer, *Works*, vol. 1, *Sanctorum Communio*, 155 (emphasis in original).
21. Bonhoeffer, *Ethics*, 198.
22. Bonhoeffer, *Ethics*, 200.
23. Scherer and Bevans, eds., "Christian Freedom and Liberation," in *New Directions*, 124.

8:4

Prophetic Witness

*"You are the light of the world. A city built on a hill cannot be hidden...
In the same way, let your light shine before others, so that they may see your
good works and give glory to your Father in heaven."*

—MATTHEW 5:14–16

The prophetic witness of the church is not grounded in what the church is, but rather what it needs to become. This has three important dimensions.

First, the church does not have the authority to decide on its own the changes that are needed in our world. Because the church is the fruit of God's salvific work in Christ through the Spirit, its identity is *bound* up with Christ. As Bonhoeffer puts it, "Jesus Christ is at once himself and his Church," and the community of faith is the "fellowship of the baptized" and is therefore "identical with Christ's own body."[24]

This means that the church is to *be* what Christ *is*—and Christ is the great prophet, who declares the will and purposes of God, denouncing all forms of oppression, and championing the cause of the poor and oppressed.

Second, in seeking to be like Christ and to be bound to Christ, the church needs constant revitalization, forgiveness, and healing. Bonhoeffer points out that the "church of the gospel is a church that is always penitent."[25] Moreover, because the church is a prophetic community in Christ, it needs to hear "God's protest against us."[26] Bonhoeffer was all too aware of how far the church in Germany had strayed due to Hitler's influence and how it had become a compromised community of faith.

We can learn from Bonhoeffer's insight, for the global church today has become weak in community formation and lacking in discipleship,

---

24. Bonhoeffer, *Cost of Discipleship*, 216.
25. Bonhoeffer, *Works*, vol. 12, *Berlin 1932–1933*, 284.
26. Bonhoeffer, *Works*, vol. 12, 441.

spiritual practices, and mission. This lack of formation undermines the biblical and theological vision of the body of Christ, an impoverished situation that calls us to hear God's protest against us. For the gospel teaches us that God is rich in mercy and is constantly seeking us out to chastise us and to draw us back into the fullness of grace. God's unwavering invitation is for us to *hear* the good news and then to *embrace* it.

Third, when the community of faith is empowered in these ways, it can live an embodied gospel as a prophetic community as it seeks to proclaim God's will and purposes for the world. As a community of word and deed, the church can become a seed of the kingdom of God by living as a sign, servant, and sacrament of God's reign.

Yet such prophetic witness is costly and may call the faith community to follow a path of suffering and martyrdom. In Bonhoeffer's life and death, he embodied the call to a "daily dying of . . . Christians" as well as a call to "suffer in a representative capacity" for the sake of Christ.[27]

The church today needs to find new courage in order to follow this path in our world. While our task as Christians is to *conserve* what is good in our world, we are also called to *challenge* all that is death-dealing in society by pointing to God's way and wisdom as we seek to live a life of forgiveness, peace, and well-being for all.

> *Nowadays this is the way*
> *everyone loves himself or herself,*
> *people wish to live with God in consolations and repose,*
> *in wealth and power . . .*
> *but God knows there are few of us who want to live as persons*
> *with his humanity, or want to carry his cross with him . . .*
> *and pay humanity's debt to the full.*[28]

---

27. Bonhoeffer, *Cost of Discipleship*, 219–20.

28. From Hadewijch (thirteenth-century Beguine). Quoted in Ringma and Alexander, eds., *Of Martyrs, Monks, and Mystics*, 182.

8:5

Discipleship Service

For the Son of Man came not to be served but to serve, and to give his life a ransom for many.

—Mark 10:45

We can describe discipleship service as everything that flows out of our *relationship* with Christ as we seek to live, work, witness, and serve in fidelity to the *way* of Christ. It is all that we offer *in* Christ, *in the way of* Christ, and *for* Christ.

Since we follow Christ as the normative person for our lives, and since his life was given wholly for the salvation, healing, and restoration of all humanity, we can trust that whatever we offer to another in the way of Christ is deeply and truly *good*.

Bonhoeffer celebrated and lived out such a life of discipleship service, pointing out that we should not be afraid of the fact that God is drawing us "into partnership," nor of the fact that God "can do with us whatever he wants."[29] For God's way is a way of grace that is empowered by the Spirit, and so when God calls us, we can trust God to lead us and give us faith and perseverance.

Bonhoeffer also reminds us that "there is no community with Jesus that is not at the same time *a call to service*."[30] We can trust that any service offered in the name of Jesus is inspired by the Holy Spirit, for as Bonhoeffer writes, "only in the possession of the Holy Spirit can the work of Jesus be done."[31]

---

29. Bonhoeffer, *Works*, vol. 10, *Barcelona, Berlin, New York 1928–1931*, 503.

30. Bonhoeffer, *Works*, vol. 15, *Theological Education Underground 1937–1940*, 544 (emphasis in original).

31. Bonhoeffer, *Works*, vol. 15, 544.

Moreover, Bonhoeffer insists that Christ himself, the Living Word, "can only be grasped by the Spirit."[32] Therefore, all that we seek to do in the name of Christ must be enabled by the Spirit, for all "holy work... lies with the Holy Spirit."[33]

When we serve others in the *way of* Christ, inspired by the Beatitudes and the winsomeness of the brooding and life-giving Spirit, we breathe a gentle good into the world that can permeate every dimension of life.

We can trust that this is the case, even though Christians are often a "hidden" presence of good in the world, and our work seldom—and sometimes never—swims into the public view. Yet throughout the world, Christian women and men are continually praying for their neighbors and for major global issues and concerns while also seeking the well-being of their families and friends, serving the church, and working for the betterment of society. Christian service might range from practical care for one's needy neighbor to working on scientific projects that make food production more effective and the planet more sustainable.

In following the call to carry out discipleship service in the way of Christ, it is important to remember that we are not fulfilling a duty, but rather responding to an invitation to be who Christ has forged us to become by the Spirit. Our service *in* and *for* Christ is always an overflow of the life of grace that we have received by the Spirit as well as a manifestation of our natural giftings and training.

With Bonhoeffer, we can celebrate how the God who created us and loves us is always seeking to use *all* of who we are—our personality, passions, and capacities—for God's kingdom purposes in blessing and renewing the whole world.

To follow Jesus Christ
implies continual conversion in one's own life
as one seeks to act in ways
which are consonant with the
justice, forgiveness, and love of God's reign.[34]

---

32. Bonhoeffer, *Works*, vol. 9, *Young Bonhoeffer, 1918–1927*, 340.
33. Bonhoeffer, *Works*, vol. 9, 334.
34. Scherer and Bevans, eds., "To the Ends of the Earth," in *New Directions*, 134.

8:6

Power of Hope

Happy are those whose help is the God of Jacob,
whose hope is in the Lord their God,
who made heaven and earth, . . .
who executes justice for the oppressed . . .

—Psalm 146:5–7

Some people think that hope is a form of escapism, particularly if we are hoping that someone else will do something on our behalf. From this perspective, hope in God simply gives us permission to renege on our own personal responsibility.

Yet this is not the heartbeat of Christian hope. Although Christian hope does look to God as its source, inspiration, and direction, it comes *home* within a person's heart and mind. As God's hope becomes our hope, we are each called to become more deeply involved in the world and to *live* our hope as fully as we can.

Inspired by God, Christian hope always leads us beyond the present status quo. When we realize that the world *as it is* does not have the last word, we can begin to perceive that the world can be changed. In this way, Christian hope is both prophetic and eschatological, always seeking to reflect the new creation that *can be* in Christ. Such hope is a sign that the powers of the age to come are already working amongst us.

The Word of God contains this prophetic and eschatological hope, for it is always pointing us toward what God will *yet* do in God's final future. The life and work of Christ also contains such hope, for the salvation of Christ is not only for this life, but also for the life to come. And the Holy Spirit inspires and sustains this life-giving hope within us.

Thus Bonhoeffer pleads for us to give the Holy Spirit "full space within us" so that "the entire fullness of the Holy Spirit" can "unfold" and "ripen" within us.[35]

Bonhoeffer also warns those who follow Christ not to seek power, but to *live* in hope, since power can so easily blunt our life of repentance until we can no longer "discern . . . our own evil in the cross of Jesus Christ."[36] As a consequence, "power, success, the development of strength" eventually become "our gods."[37] Though Bonhoeffer insists that the faith community "should have hope," he acknowledges that all too often we "are grasping for power."[38]

Bonhoeffer describes the hope that characterizes Christian witness when he writes, "I lay on the floor in the darkness [of my cell] with little hope of coming through the attack safely."[39] He acknowledges that his hope for marriage with Maria "lies more on the horizon of hope than in the realm of possession."[40] And he says that his "greatest hope" is that he will ever be with his friend, Eberhard, again.[41] While he speaks of the "bitter bliss of waiting" and "of doing without,"[42] he also celebrates that God will lead his people from "death to life."[43] Thus Bonhoeffer's hope was grounded in the nature of God, who is and will always be faithful.

Similarly, our Christian hope rests in the promises of God, who continues to unfold—often in unexpected ways—the purposes of Christ for redeeming and restoring the whole world. At the same time, we live with ongoing faith, hope, and expectation for what will *yet* transpire when God will bring about the new heavens and a new earth.

> *The Christian faith is by its very nature*
> *a missionary faith.*
> *It is therefore intrinsic to the Christian church to always wish to cross frontiers*
> *and share its gospel with others. . . .*
> *There is . . . a strange and wonderful paradox here.*

---

35. Bonhoeffer, *Works*, vol. 16, *Conspiracy and Imprisonment 1940–1945*, 628.
36. Bonhoeffer, *Works*, vol. 16, 46.
37. Bonhoeffer, *Works*, vol. 16, 638.
38. Bonhoeffer, *Works*, vol. 12, *Berlin 1932–1933*, 444.
39. Bonhoeffer, *Letters and Papers*, 149.
40. Bonhoeffer, *Letters and Papers*, 160.
41. Bonhoeffer, *Letters and Papers*, 223.
42. Bonhoeffer, *Works*, vol. 10, *Barcelona, Berlin, New York 1928–1931*, 542.
43. Bonhoeffer, *Works*, vol. 10, 489.

Engaging Society

*On the one hand, we are to give our all
to the evangelization of God's world, and yet on the other hand,
we are given the assurance that it is God's work
and that God will do it.*[44]

---

44. Scherer and Bevans, eds., "Stuttgart Consultation," in *New Directions*, 68.

9

Celebrating the Good in Our World

Introduction

For much of my life, I have been around radical Christians, and there is much to admire in their vision for a better world, willingness to work for the good in hope, courage to proclaim truth to power, and resilience in the face of suffering. But radical Christians can also be overly idealistic, unfairly critical of others, and over time their projects can run out of steam. Another difficulty is that radical Christians often don't give much attention to the "ordinary" realities and structures of everyday life.

Bonhoeffer is a helpful guide, for even though he practices radical alternatives in his engagement of the world, he also maintains a vision for continuing the ordinary realities of life—family, work, church, governance, among others. This is both refreshing and challenging, for his example calls us to live a more dynamic dialectic, embracing both church and community, Word and Spirit, prophecy and maintenance.

In Bonhoeffer's *Ethics*, he writes that we are called to live "the Christian life under . . . four mandates of God": labor, marriage, governance, and church.[1] He goes on to point out that "the Christian . . . is at once laborer, partner in a marriage, and subject to a government."[2] Because the Christian is called to live these mandates for the sake of Christ and in solidarity

---

1. Bonhoeffer, *Ethics*, 204.
2. Bonhoeffer, *Ethics*, 208.

with his or her neighbor, the Christian is both a citizen and a person in Christ.

Within this context, Bonhoeffer situates his important discussion about the relationship between the *penultimate* and the *ultimate*. By *penultimate*, he is referring to what we would call ordinary life—all that has not found its fulfillment in the grace and renewal of Christ, but is life nonetheless under the gaze and purposes of God. As Bonhoeffer puts it, "the fallen creation is still the creation, and... sinful man [woman] still remains man [woman]."[3] Because life must not be negated or squandered in any way, Christians should do everything they can to maintain and enhance ordinary life.

Yet for the Christian, the *ultimate* is also important, though this does not refer to a vision of utopia or heaven. Rather, Bonhoeffer asserts that the "Christian life is the dawning of the ultimate *in* me," which he describes as "the life of Jesus Christ *in* me."[4]

In describing the relationship between the penultimate and ultimate aspects of life, Bonhoeffer argues that the "penultimate must be preserved" for the sake of the ultimate, even while the "ultimate... determines the penultimate."[5] To put this more simply, Bonhoeffer is proposing that the whole scope of civic life must be sustained and enhanced so that the power of the gospel may penetrate every dimension of life. He goes on to say that the penultimate has already been provided for in the death and resurrection of Christ, for "in Jesus Christ the reality of God entered into the reality of the world."[6] As such, the world belongs "wholly to Christ."[7]

At the same time, Bonhoeffer asserts that the Christian "stands... wholly in the world" and is called to do everything possible through prayer and service to preserve the world *for* the ultimate, since the "gospel... is addressed to the whole world."[8] Bonhoeffer makes the further point that the revelation of God in Jesus Christ "occupies space within the world."[9]

For Christians, this means that we live a double-calling of maintaining an ordinary life as citizens in society while also maintaining the dynamics

---

3. Bonhoeffer, *Ethics*, 138.
4. Bonhoeffer, *Ethics*, 141 (emphasis in original).
5. Bonhoeffer, *Ethics*, 133.
6. Bonhoeffer, *Ethics*, 192.
7. Bonhoeffer, *Ethics*, 198.
8. Bonhoeffer, *Ethics*, 197, 198.
9. Bonhoeffer, *Ethics*, 199.

of our life of faith in the radical and transformative power of Jesus Christ through the Holy Spirit. In living this dialectic, we affirm both dimensions of life rather than negating one or the other. In other words, we do not become so concerned and enamored with ordinary life that we neglect our life of faith, nor do we become so heavenly minded that we neglect the world.

This calls for a spirituality that is both concerned with the world and shaped by a heavenly hope, a focus that is both transcendent and incarnational. In this spirituality, we work for justice, beauty, and the common good, and we are sustained by practices of prayer and contemplation.

Bonhoeffer, a surprising radical, plunges us wholly into the salvific work of Christ, which casts us to bear the light and hope of Christ into every domain in our world—earth-keeping, good governance, human flourishing, peacemaking, and care for the poor. As we grasp this vision, we will need to be sustained continually by the nurturing Spirit.

9:1

The Gift of Family

"And in your descendants all the families of the earth shall be blessed."
—Acts 3:25

It is well known that Dietrich Bonhoeffer came from a well-to-do, cultured family, and this background played an important part in shaping him and sustaining him to the very end.[10] It is also well known that Bonhoeffer had a deep love for his family of origin. As he writes in a letter from prison, "in such hard-pressed times, it is such a treasure to have such a large, close-knit family in which everyone trusts and supports one another."[11]

Growing up, Bonhoeffer was encouraged to develop his gifts and abilities and was given room to make personal educational and vocational choices. To the surprise of his family, he desired to engage in theological studies and support the church.

God's gifts to humanity are both natural and salvific. The natural gifts include the divine mandates of the earth, life, family, work, and governance. In celebrating these divine mandates, Bonhoeffer exclaims, "what treasures a good family life, good parents, right and truth, humanity and education and tradition are"![12] He also stresses that we should have a deep concern for "an authentic worldly order under God's command."[13] These gifts all flow out of God's providential concern for the world.

At the same time, God's salvific gifts include our redemption and healing in Christ through the Spirit. Having received these gifts, we can live out God's purposes for the world—forgiveness, reconciliation, peacemaking, and the hope of God's final future—in the normal fabric of daily life.

10. For something of the family history, see Bethge, *Dietrich Bonhoeffer*, 3–65.
11. Bonhoeffer, *Works*, vol. 8, *Letters and Papers from Prison*, 110.
12. Bonhoeffer, *Works*, vol, 16, *Conspiracy and Imprisonment 1940–1945*, 365.
13. Bonhoeffer, *Works*, vol. 16, 532.

Throughout Bonhoeffer's writings, he returns to these matters and develops some important concepts. First, he emphasizes that while God is concerned about each of us individually, God is also concerned about the social bonds that we create and maintain. Bonhoeffer notes that "God intended for us to live among nations, families, and friendships," and he goes on to explain that the various forms of our life together should be marked by being "respectful, honorable, and reverential."[14]

In this context, he argues that there is "a will of God with a *people*," not just with us as "individuals."[15] Thus God's goodness and judgment can be applied to us as "collective persons [*Kollektivpersonen*]."[16] In other words, we must not live self-absorbed lives, as we have both individual and corporate responsibilities. Moreover, Christians should not only be concerned with saving individuals, as they also need to be concerned with restoring the social fabric of life and its institutions.

Second, Bonhoeffer makes it clear that we should have a deeper understanding of the connection between the "natural" and the "spiritual." He argues that the language of family is also applied to God (Father and Son) as well as the church (brothers and sisters).[17] As he puts it, "one might call the church . . . a family moved by the Spirit."[18] Thus first and foremost, Bonhoeffer does not see the faith community as an institution, but as a mystical-relational body. As the mystical body of Christ, the church is a relational community that shares a common Lord, common faith, and common purpose.

In our day of rampant, atomistic individualism, Bonhoeffer's voice is important. As Christians, we need to be attentive both to the corporate life of the family and church as well as the social configurations of society, for God's purposes are always personal, relational, and institutional.

> *Bring your joy into all families;*
> *strengthen and deliver those in childbirth,*
> *watch over children and guide the young,*
> *bring reconciliation*
> *to those in discord*
> *and peace to those in stress.*[19]

---

14. Bonhoeffer, *Works*, vol. 9, *Young Bonhoeffer, 1918–1927*, 535.
15. Bonhoeffer, *Works*, vol. 1, *Sanctorum Communio*, 119 (emphasis in original).
16. Bonhoeffer, *Works*, vol. 1, 284.
17. Bonhoeffer, *Works*, vol. 1, 263.
18. Bonhoeffer, *Works*, vol. 1, 264.
19. *Common Worship*, 113.

9:2

The Gift of Learning

> *... learn to do good;*
> *seek justice,*
> *rescue the oppressed,*
> *defend the orphan,*
> *plead for the widow.*
>
> —Isaiah 1:17

Bonhoeffer came from a very gifted family, where creativity, education, music, and other aspects of culture were encouraged and appreciated. Indeed, by the age of twenty-one, young Dietrich had completed his doctorate in theology!

But for Bonhoeffer, learning was multidimensional. Though he obviously devoted himself to intellectual learning and studying theology, he also learned much from his family about family life, social realities, and politics. In his early involvement with the church, he learned through his pastoral responsibilities, which led him to develop empathy, care, and commitment. He was also on a steep learning curve as he wrestled with his country's political trajectory under Hitler and sought to develop a theological critique while playing a part in the formation of the Confessing Church. But he had even more to learn when he began to train clergy in a semi-monastic setting—and then when he joined the direct opposition to Hitler.

In *Letters and Papers from Prison,* it is clear that he continued to wrestle with many theological, ethical, missional, and sociocultural issues until his death. From this, we can say that Bonhoeffer was a lifelong learner, who learned from a wide range of disciplines—theology, philosophy, sociology, as well as praxis (his involvement in the issues of his time).

But Bonhoeffer's familial formation, formal education, and wider learning always had a christological center, which was not only informational, but also existential and ontological. For Bonhoeffer, Christ was both the redeemer and the icon of a new humanity, the savior and the Lord of history. Thus Bonhoeffer sought to live with the personal comfort of knowing Christ as his savior and friend, and he also saw Christ as the normative being for all humanity, including the political order.

In Bonhoeffer's learning, he was not simply seeking the propositions of theology, but "what Jesus Christ himself wants of us."[20] He insisted that such knowing had to be rooted in an "attachment to his [Christ's] person."[21] Moreover, it had to involve a "life of discipleship" that issued forth in "practical obedience."[22]

The pursuit of knowing "what Jesus himself wants"[23] led Bonhoeffer into a life of struggle, learning, faith, repentance, courage, witness, and service. His knowledge was not based on static certainty, but a dynamic future. And he continually sought the ways of the Spirit while listening and responding to wisdom from Scripture as well as what was happening in his society and culture.

In all of Bonhoeffer's learning, he sought to be—and more fully become—the person he was created to be in and through Christ. His learning involved prayer, which he described as "the supreme instance of the hidden character of the Christian life."[24] It also involved living a cruciform life, as he believed that the "cross [is] laid on every Christian."[25] And it involved taking upon himself suffering for the sake of others as a "vicarious activity."[26]

As Bonhoeffer teaches us, learning to be a follower of Christ is a daily challenge and a lifelong activity. And as we learn the pains, challenges, and dysfunctionalities of our age, we will be confronted by distressing realities. But when we learn to keep responding in faith and hope, we live as a sign of the God who is with us in Christ through the Spirit, whose "kindly yoke" we must embrace.[27]

God of our pilgrimage,
who hast willed that the gate of mercy

---

20. Bonhoeffer, *Cost of Discipleship*, 29.
21. Bonhoeffer, *Cost of Discipleship*, 49.
22. Bonhoeffer, *Cost of Discipleship*, 66, 63.
23. Bonhoeffer, *Cost of Discipleship*, 29.
24. Bonhoeffer, *Cost of Discipleship*, 146.
25. Bonhoeffer, *Cost of Discipleship*, 79.
26. Bonhoeffer, *Cost of Discipleship*, 220.
27. Bonhoeffer, *Cost of Discipleship*, 31.

should stand open for those who trust in thee:
look upon us with thy favor
that we, following in the path of thy will,
may never wander from the way of life;
through Jesus Christ our Lord.[28]

---

28. *Common Worship*, 486.

9:3

The Gift of Creativity

When you send forth your spirit, they are created;
and you renew the face of the ground.

—Psalm 104:30

God has given us the gifts of creation and the blessings of redemption. We have also received much goodness through the church and from culture and society.

God's presence abides in the church through word and sacrament, and it resides in the world through God's providential upholding of all things and the gifts of family, work, and governance. Though God's presence is often "hidden" and can only be discerned with the eyes of faith, nothing in the world has been abandoned, since the whole world has been caught up in the redemptive work of Christ.

While we are confronted daily with threats to human well-being, social harmony, and justice, we also experience human creativity whenever anyone seeks to restore and make whole what is broken and dysfunctional.

This work of creative restoration takes place at all levels of society—the personal and communal, the spiritual and economic, in both the family and the political order. In the midst of this work, we receive many gifts of beauty, art, music, and other expressions of human creativity that make our lives joyful and fill us with gratitude.

Simply put, God's creativity and beauty are embryonic in humanity, for we are all made in the image and likeness of God. Everywhere, in every sphere of life, this creativity can bubble to the surface. Such ongoing, generative creativity is essential, for everything we create is also marked by decay, and so restoration is a fundamental characteristic of creativity.

Bonhoeffer understood that every aspect of life in Germany was under threat of Nazi ideology, because the state that was supposed to maintain "the order of [the] preservation of life"[29] was failing in its God-given responsibility. As he saw it, this failure stemmed from the fact that "the world ... makes its own gods."[30] Thus he knew that God's creative work of restoration had to proceed on every front—in the renewal of the church, the reconfiguration of the political order, and the complete restoration of society.

In response to the profound aberration of human well-being during these dark days in Germany, Bonhoeffer became involved in many creative responses. On the political front, he sought the support of church leaders in the United Kingdom to back the resistance movement in Germany. But his primary focus was to seek renewal within the church, which he criticized for being a "religiously inclined ... people," where God is often seen as "a plaything."[31] He longed to see the faith community restored by a vision of what the church was intended to be through the work of Christ and the purposes of God.

Bonhoeffer believed that the church could be renewed by the power of the gospel and the Holy Spirit if it was willing to embrace costly discipleship and sacrificial service as a sign of the inbreaking of the kingdom of God. He describes the faith community as a "church of sinners" that "lives only by ... grace."[32] Yet he insists that the faith community can give "shock to the world" and contribute to the "establishment of a new order of values."[33] In journeying towards this future reign of God, where there will be justice, peace, and well-being for all, he calls the church to live out of a "most profound solidarity *with* the world."[34]

Bonhoeffer's creative voice continues to challenge us today, both in the tired, religious Christianity of the Western world as well as the church in the Majority world, which is groaning under the yoke of poverty and dysfunctional governance.

> *O Lord, save thy people and bless thine inheritance.*
> *Govern them and lift them up for ever ...*
> *Vouchsafe, O Lord, to keep us this day without sin.*

---

29. Bonhoeffer, *Works,* vol. 12, *Berlin 1932–1933,* 293.
30. Bonhoeffer, *Works,* vol. 13, *London 1933–1935,* 362.
31. Bonhoeffer, *Works,* vol. 12, *Berlin 1932–1933,* 263.
32. Bonhoeffer, *Works,* vol. 13, *London 1933–1935,* 393.
33. Bonhoeffer, *Works,* vol. 13, 402–3.
34. Bonhoeffer, *Works,* vol. 12, *Berlin 1932–1933,* 289 (emphasis in original).

In the Shadow of a Rugged Cross

O Lord, have mercy upon us, have mercy upon us.
O Lord, let thy mercy lighten upon us, as our trust is in thee.[35]

---

35. *Common Worship*, 806.

9:4

A New Humanity: Bound by Love

He has abolished the law with its commandments and ordinances, so that he might create in himself one new humanity . . .

—EPHESIANS 2:15

Bonhoeffer lived during a time when his society was adopting a political ideology that sought to create a sociopolitical entity based on racial and ethnic identity, where one was either included as a pure Aryan or excluded as less than human. This ideology led to the extermination of millions of Jews as well as Gypsies, gays, communists, and people with disabilities. Of course, those who opposed the regime were also eradicated.

Bonhoeffer insists that when the state oversteps "its task" and makes "itself lord," it must be resisted and "disobeyed for the sake of conscience and for the sake of the Lord."[36] Thus Bonhoeffer felt that he must reject this vision of a society based on racial purity and the coercive power of the state, as Christ had given him a very different vision of society and the world.[37] He argues that because "the whole world has already been turned upside down by the work of Jesus Christ," the redemptive freedom of Christ is available for *all* humanity.[38]

Bonhoeffer first articulated this vision of redemptive freedom in Christ in relation to the church. Because the faith community is a "fellowship of the baptized," it is "identical with Christ's own body."[39] And because the church "is the 'New Man' [Woman]" in Christ, the new man or woman in Christ "cannot be a solitary individual."[40] In other words, though we re-

---

36. Bonhoeffer, *Works*, vol. 16, *Conspiracy and Imprisonment 1940–1945*, 517.
37. For a helpful articulation, see Green, *Bonhoeffer*.
38. Bonhoeffer, *Cost of Discipleship*, 234.
39. Bonhoeffer, *Cost of Discipleship*, 216.
40. Bonhoeffer, *Cost of Discipleship*, 217, 218.

tain our personhood in Christ, we become a distinctive "collective" of love, fellowship, and service as a prefiguration of what God is seeking to create in the world.

Moreover, Bonhoeffer argues that this faith community in Christ does not exist for itself, but wholly for God's purpose of restoring all humanity—including Jews, Gypsies, gays, communists, and those with disabilities (the very people that Hitler's ideology excluded). Christians are called to live out this quest for freedom, peace, and justice for *all* under God's beneficent lordship of redemption, inclusion, and hospitality, because "Christians always see other men [women] as brethren [sisters] to whom Christ comes."[41]

Bonhoeffer also insists that the faith community, which lives as a seed of the kingdom of God, must bind itself in solidarity "to the earth, to misery, to hunger, to death."[42] Thus for Bonhoeffer, Christ had *bound* him to family, friends, the church community, those he joined in resisting Hitler, his fellow prisoners, all neighbors, and most particularly those who were excluded and suffering.

The particularity of Christ creates a *new universality* that calls us to see our social bonds not in terms of race, politics, or religion, but as gifts of the incarnation and redemption of Christ, who is forging a new humanity. Most simply, this new humanity is to live in love for God, neighbor, and the whole world.

> *Heavenly Father,*
> *you have called us in the Body of your Son Jesus Christ*
> *to continue his work of reconciliation*
> *and reveal you to the world:*
> *forgive us the sins that tear us apart;*
> *give us courage to overcome our fears*
> *and to seek that unity which is your gift and your will;*
> *through Jesus Christ your Son our Lord.*[43]

---

41. Bonhoeffer, *Cost of Discipleship*, 163.
42. Bonhoeffer, *Works*, vol. 12, *Berlin 1932–1933*, 289.
43. *Common Worship*, 104.

9:5

A Global and Ecumenical Church

We do not want you to be unaware, brothers and sisters, of the affliction we experienced in Asia; for we were so utterly, unbearably crushed that we despaired of life itself.

—2 Corinthians 1:8

Very early in Bonhoeffer's theological career, he became involved with the international ecumenical movement. This orientation formed a stark contrast with the Protestant church in Germany, which was being turned "into a Reich church for Christians of the Aryan race."[44]

Bonhoeffer and others resisted this development in Germany, insisting that church affiliation is not determined by "blood . . . [and] race," but "by the Holy Spirit and baptism."[45] Moreover, he argued that in obedience to God's lordship, the faith community must resist the state and "accuse the state of offences against morality."[46]

Bonhoeffer's resistance involved a long and discouraging struggle, and he often despaired about how the newly formed church of resistance, the Confessing Church, could respond. Eventually, Bonhoeffer became part of the Abwehr—the German Military Intelligence—and sought to harness support for the opposition movement within Germany from his international contacts within the ecumenical movement.

Bonhoeffer's involvements with the Abwehr and the ecumenical movement highlight an important reality, which is that any creative renewal movement cannot be bound by parochial concerns alone. If we are seeking the restoration of an urban poor community in Manila, we need to engage the sociopolitical issues within the Philippines as well as the impact

---

44. Bonhoeffer, *Works*, vol. 12, *Berlin 1932–1933*, 420.
45. Bonhoeffer, *Works*, vol. 12, 419.
46. Bonhoeffer, *Works*, vol. 12, 363.

of international markets, trade agreements, the International Monetary Fund, and the banking sector.

Bonhoeffer was unsuccessful in gaining support from international church leaders. And his involvement with the Abwehr led to his arrest, imprisonment, and execution. Yet his work with both highlights an important ecumenical dimension of the church.

While a parish church exists as a local faith community within a particular neighborhood, it is also part of a wider denomination or network of churches. In the ecumenical vision, local churches and their denominations can also be part of a global network. A church can transcend local, national, and denominational boundaries by grounding its ecclesiastical identity in Christ. Moreover, it can draw inspiration from the Trinity, which exemplifies unity in diversity and can provide a vision for a spiritual and practical coinherence within the global community of faith.

When we live a life of faith in Jesus as the Lord of the world, we break out of our ecclesiastical ghettoes and are plunged into the vast expanses of a universal faith and a global church. We need to recover this vision of the church in our time so that we can overcome our party politics and racial divisions on the home front and rethink our loyalties within the global realities of our world.

Bonhoeffer shows us that being a Christian is our primary loyalty, above all others—and this loyalty will call us to question national patriotism. As Christians, we might not be able to support everything that our government is doing. Moreover, we might be called to support Christians in other countries where our country is doing harm.

Our solidarity in Christ is a social bond that can and should supersede both our ethnicity and nationality, for as Christians, we belong to a global "third" race.

> *Almighty God,*
> *by whose providence thy servant John the Baptist*
> *was wonderfully born,*
> *and sent to prepare the way of thy Son our Savior,*
> *by preaching repentance:*
> *make us so to follow his doctrine and holy life,*
> *that we may truly repent according to his preaching*
> *and, after his example,*
> *constantly speak the truth, boldly rebuke vice,*
> *and patiently suffer for the truth's sake*
> *through Jesus Christ our Lord.*[47]

---

47. *Common Worship*, 507.

9:6

Future Hope

*Hope deferred makes the heart sick,
but a desire fulfilled is a tree of life.*

—Proverbs 13:12

Bonhoeffer neither sought to escape from the difficulties of life, nor was he unrealistic about the great challenges the church would face in bringing about a world of restoration and justice. Yet despite all the chaos of war during his time, he continued to envisage life under God's lordship, when peace would reign and there would be justice and well-being for all.

In a sermon Bonhoeffer prepared in prison for the baptism of newborn Dietrich Wilhelm Rudiger Bethge, Bonhoeffer suggests that in the midst of war, it is best to "hope rather than plan."[48] Yet he goes on to say that the time will come when the "rising generation" will again make it possible "to plan, build up, and shape a new and better life."[49]

Bonhoeffer continually looked forward to a post-war world. At the same time, he looked forward to the time when he and his fiancé, Maria von Wedemeyer, could marry. He speaks of his hope in "my and Maria's wedding day," but he later acknowledges how hard it is that life with Maria "lies more on the horizon of hope" rather than "in the realm of possession."[50]

Bonhoeffer's letters to Maria during the years of his imprisonment are marked by hope.[51] In one letter, he writes, "We've now been waiting for each other for almost two years, dearest Maria. Don't lose heart!"[52] But he also reveals the struggles of separation, speaking of a faith that "endures

---

48. Bonhoeffer, *Letters and Papers from Prison*, 297.
49. Bonhoeffer, *Letters and Papers*, 297.
50. Bonhoeffer, *Letters and Papers*, 30, 160.
51. Bismarck and Kabitz, eds., *Love Letters from Cell 92*.
52. Bismarck and Kabitz, eds., *Love Letters from Cell 92*, 228.

in the world" and "remains true to that world in spite all the hardships it brings."[53]

In these letters, Bonhoeffer celebrates Maria's love for him, declaring that their future marriage "must be a 'yes' to God's earth."[54] He also speaks of their love within the frame of surrendering to God's ways, insisting that "our love and our marriage will derive eternal strength from this time of trial."[55] And later, he remarks that "God is forever upsetting our plans, but only in order to fulfill his own, better plans for us."[56]

Bonhoeffer attributes his hope to Christ. He speaks of the Holy Spirit putting "Christ in our hearts, creating faith and hope."[57] He goes on to say that hope is the "most sacred treasure" of the faith community, and it is "in hope [that] the church grows strong."[58]

Yet Bonhoeffer also acknowledges that a person might be afraid of God. He confesses that "God might draw us into partnership and do with us whatever he wants," and so we might be afraid of "being seized and called upon by the infinite."[59] Nonetheless, Bonhoeffer insists that the grace of Christ overcomes these fears, for when we look at the cross of Christ, our gaze opens to the hope "when God will make everything new again."[60]

Strengthened by the cross of Christ, Bonhoeffer can confess with both faith and hope that "God will cause grace and compassion to radiate over the dark guilt of our century and the human race."[61]

> *I worried that my vision would fail*
> *and I would be left to myself.*
> *I hoped with confidence in his endless love,*
> *which I knew would protect me under his mercy*
> *and bring me to eternal blessedness.*

---

53. Bismarck and Kabitz, eds., *Love Letters from Cell 92*, 48.
54. Bismarck and Kabitz, eds., *Love Letters from Cell 92*, 48.
55. Bismarck and Kabitz, eds., *Love Letters from Cell 92*, 49.
56. Bismarck and Kabitz, eds., *Love Letters from Cell 92*, 186.
57. Bonhoeffer, *Works*, vol. 1, *Sanctorum Communio*, 165.
58. Bonhoeffer, *Works*, vol. 1, 289.
59. Bonhoeffer, *Works*, vol. 10, *Barcelona, Berlin, New York 1928–1931*, 503.
60. Bonhoeffer, *Works*, vol. 10, 358.
61. Bonhoeffer, *Works*, vol. 10, 359.

Celebrating the Good in Our World

My joy and confident hope in his merciful protection
gave me such comfort
that mourning and fear were not too painful.[62]

---

62. From Julian of Norwich (c. 1342–1413). Quoted in Ringma and Alexander, eds., *Of Martyrs, Monks, and Mystics*, 381.

10

A Spirituality of Hope

Introduction

As human creatures, we are shaped by our socialization and historicity and become acutely aware of our limitations. At the same time, we continually engage in looking ahead, projecting ourselves into the future. This forward-looking orientation suggests that hope seems to be a fundamental aspect of our humanity.

While some of our collective hopes might look like daydreaming or wishful thinking, most of us are longing for greater self-fulfillment and signs that things will become better and more just in our world.

The theme of hope occurs throughout the biblical narratives, which remind us that God is *with* us and God is also *ahead* of us, beckoning us into God's unfolding presence and goodness in the world. As we seek to follow God in our present circumstances, we trust that God will continue to be present and provide for us in the future. In other words, God *is,* and God *will be.*

More specifically, Christian hope is rooted in what God has already done in Christ and also in what God is yet to do through the life-giving empowerment of the Holy Spirit. This hope calls us to live the *yet* and *not-yet* nature of Christian existence. We are in Christ, but we are also in the world. We have come home in Christ, but we are still pilgrims on the way. We have eternal life in Christ, and we still await its fuller manifestation.

A Spirituality of Hope

There is nothing static about Christian hope, for it is constantly being challenged and contested. Sometimes our hope fades, and we might find ourselves walking through the dark night of the soul. And when we experience times of temptation, we sometimes lose our way.

Another aspect of Christian hope is that it is not a product of self-enhancement, but a gift from God that is rooted in God's promises and the empowering of the Holy Spirit. At the same time, Christian hope is not simply a personal gift, for it is rooted in our identity as being part of the body of Christ. Though our hope may fade in times of discouragement, the hope of our sisters and brothers in the faith community can sustain us.

Bonhoeffer explains that Christians point the way toward "a new humanity which, in hope, overcomes the history of sin and death."[1] We cannot produce this newness, for it is rooted in Christ alone. Bonhoeffer speaks of the God "who set the beginning" of our new life "once through his forgiving and renewing word in Jesus Christ, that is, in my baptism, in my rebirth, in my conversion."[2] Moreover, this word of Christ can only be "effectively brought to the heart of the hearers by the Spirit."[3]

Thus Christian hope is not utopian, but dialectical. Though sin and idolatry persist in our world, the grace of God through the Spirit continues to erupt and intervene among us.

On the one hand, Bonhoeffer argues that "God's love for the world does not consist of bringing an end to wars, and taking poverty, need, persecution, and catastrophes of all kinds, away from us."[4] On the other hand, he insists that Christians are all called to pray and work for reconciliation, shalom, and well-being, because our "Yes to God demands [our] No to all injustice, . . . evil, . . . lies, . . . oppression, and violation of the weak and the poor . . ."[5]

Christian hope is disruptive, for it does not accept the status quo or settle for "the way things are." Thus Christian hope is always restless, longing for the good that can *yet* be. At the same time, this longing gaze looks to God to guide, sustain, and empower the faith community to *live* the gospel through prayer and work so that that God's will might be done on earth as it is in heaven (Matt 6:10).

---

1. Bonhoeffer, *Works*, vol. 1, *Sanctorum Communio*, 63.
2. Bonhoeffer, *Works*, vol. 15, *Theological Education Underground 1937–1940*, 497.
3. Bonhoeffer, *Works*, vol. 1, *Sanctorum Communio*, 158.
4. Bonhoeffer, *Works*, vol. 15, *Theological Education Underground 1937–1940*, 558.
5. Bonhoeffer, *Works*, vol. 15, 478.

10:1

The Gift of Hope

Can any idols of the nations bring rain?
Or can the heavens give showers?
Is it not you, O Lord our God?
We set our hope on you,
for it is you who do all this.

—JEREMIAH 14:22

In our contemporary world, particularly in the West, many people are seeking to live without any reference to God, grace, or salvation, relying instead on their own self-sufficiency and autonomy. From this perspective, humanity alone is responsible for making and bettering our world, and any reference to God is seen as a cop-out on personal responsibility.

Others believe in the importance of human initiative in shaping and caring for our world and the human community, but are seeking to live this out in the wisdom of God, trusting that any good that humanity can do flows out of the goodness of God.

Bonhoeffer affirms that this is the only way to live, as it is based on God's initiative rather than our human achievement. As he puts it, "God's path to human beings" is a "much greater hope" than our path to God.[6]

We may wonder why Bonhoeffer thinks that God's initiative is better than human achievement—or why hope in God is a better hope. Part of the answer lies in Bonhoeffer's experience of the madness of Hitler's Third Reich and its attempt to become godlike. Whenever we encounter power without accountability, it becomes grotesque and demonic.

Because God's will is for the restoration and healing of the whole world, God's initiative will always point us towards greater hope. To live out

---

6. Bonhoeffer, *Works*, vol. 10, *Barcelona, Berlin, New York 1928–1931*, 483.

A Spirituality of Hope

of this hope, we must be rooted in Jesus, for through his death and resurrection he made a way for the redemption of the whole world. This way of God is all about welcome and invitation, and God's way in Christ through the Spirit renews us from within so that we can become a blessing to others. This welcoming way is depicted in the Beatitudes, which outline a way of forgiveness and peace as well as justice and freedom for the oppressed.

Moreover, Christian hope is not simply about hoping for something better, for it is grounded in the work God has *already* done in Christ as it continues to unfold in our world. In this unfolding, God seeks to work through the members of the faith community, who have been marked by the grace and goodness of God in Christ. Sustained by God's mission of grace for the world, the faith community lives as a sign and a servant of God's power, which continually seeks the restoration of all things.

But as Bonhoeffer points out, Christian hope is always a waiting hope, for it has not yet fully come. It beckons us forward, but we will not necessarily find this waiting easy. Rather, Bonhoeffer speaks of the "bitter bliss of waiting."[7]

Living such a bitter, waiting hope is a purging experience, for we will face our limitations, and we will continually long for greater trust, more earnest prayer, a chastised faith, and a deeper wonderment regarding God's way and purposes.

> *We therefore reject as a proud, self-confident dream*
> *the notion that man [woman] can ever build a utopia on earth.*
> *Our Christian confidence is that God will perfect his kingdom,*
> *and we look forward with eager anticipation to that day,*
> *and to the new heaven and earth in which righteousness will dwell*
> *and God will reign forever.*[8]

---

7. Bonhoeffer, *Works*, vol. 10, 542.
8. Stott, ed., "Lausanne Covenant," in *Making Christ Known*, 49.

10:2

The Power of Hope

To them God chose to make known how great among the Gentiles are the riches of the glory of this mystery, which is Christ in you, the hope of glory.
—COLOSSIANS 1:27

We live amidst a great diversity of peoples and cultures—and also within the particularity of who we are. But no matter how culturally different we may be from others, we share a common humanity. Moreover, from a theological perspective, we are all made in the image of God.

Being made in the image of God does not just set us apart from animals, for being human also seems to include a longing for transcendence and a hope beyond ourselves.

But the delicate membranes of hope can be shattered, and our humanity can be brutalized. Bonhoeffer experienced this amidst Hitler's regime, when so much humanity and common decency was turned upside down.

As in Bonhoeffer's time, there is much to grieve and lament in our day—abuse in families, pressure in the workplace, personal invasion from consumer culture, distortion in the media. And globally, there are so many refugees, so much poverty, so many authoritarian forms of government. There are also the specters that invade our dreams—changing empires, climate distortions, the cacophony of misinformation, our invasive surveillance societies, the persistence of war, and so much more.

Living with hope amidst these circumstances might seem like wishful thinking. For, as Bonhoeffer notes, when hope is gone "then everything is lost."[9] Yet he also asserts that "where there is still hope, there is no defeat."[10]

---

9. Bonhoeffer, *Works*, vol. 15, *Theological Education Underground 1937–1940*, 475.
10. Bonhoeffer, *Works*, vol. 15, 475.

A Spirituality of Hope

Bonhoeffer clung to hope because he believed that "life is the time of grace."[11] Moreover, his hope was rooted in his unwavering belief in the magnificence and depth of the love of God in Christ Jesus, which has a transformative power that enables our life to become "one great act of trust in God."[12]

For Bonhoeffer, hope is not just anthropological, but christological, for Christ is the source of our hope. Yet this hope is most unusual, for it is not based on pomp and power. Rather, as Bonhoeffer puts it, "God is not ashamed of human lowliness but goes right into the middle of it."[13] Therefore, "the throne of God is set not on the thrones of humankind, but in humanity's deepest abyss, in the manger."[14]

This strange way of descent leads to glory, for the way of the cross is the way to God's final future in the restoration of all things.

Bonhoeffer's hope in Christ shaped his entire life, calling him to follow the threads of this hope to the very end. As he writes, "who would want to talk about a new world and a new humanity without the hope of sharing in them oneself?"[15]

Bonhoeffer teaches us that all Christian hope is rooted in Christ, and our hope is not simply something we believe in, but a hope that we *live*—and for which we are willing to die. As he writes, "believing in God would take away our faith in all other powers."[16] And when we live this hope, we will find ourselves living against all the ideological hopes of our world.

> *We pledge ourselves to* live *under the Lordship of Christ,*
> *and to be concerned for his will and glory, and not our own. . . .*
> *We pledge ourselves to* give *with the generosity of Christ,*
> *that we may share with others what he has given to us. . . .*
> *We pledge ourselves to* serve *the needy and oppressed,*
> *and in the name of Christ to seek for them relief and justice.*[17]

---

11. Bonhoeffer, *Works*, vol. 15, 519.
12. Bonhoeffer, *Works*, vol. 13, *London 1933–1935*, 405.
13. Bonhoeffer, *Works*, vol. 13, 344.
14. Bonhoeffer, *Works*, vol. 13, 345.
15. Bonhoeffer, *Works*, vol. 13, 394.
16. Bonhoeffer, *Works*, vol. 13, 405.
17. Stott, ed., "Thailand Statement," in *Making Christ Known*, 162.

10:3

The Struggles of Hope

He breaks me down on every side, and I am gone,
he has uprooted my hope like a tree.

—JOB 19:10

The reader of this book will have concluded by now that Bonhoeffer was not a happy optimist. Yet it is equally important to perceive that he was not a pessimist either. Instead, Bonhoeffer sought to face life with an unwavering scrutiny, but also with the faith that God graciously and lovingly entered the world in Christ, and therefore God will continue to redeem and renew humanity and the whole world.

In describing the madness of his times, Bonhoeffer writes that "when one after another all the things our life depends on are taken away," we should not despair, but have courage, for "God is coming near to us."[18]

This strange way of thinking was not pious escapism, for Bonhoeffer did not believe that "redemption" was an escape "from cares, distress, fears."[19] Rather, he believed that God, in humility, had entered the brokenness of the world and humanity in order to take that sinfulness and deviance upon himself in Christ, for the sake of the world's healing and restoration. In seeking after God, he insists that the disciple of Christ "must drink the earthly cup" of suffering, because it is through loss and suffering that God's redemption draws near.[20]

Bonhoeffer devoted his life to this challenging and paradoxical hope in Christ. When all seemed lost, he was found. When things were taken away, he believed his open hands could be filled. When death seemed near, he trusted that new life would be given to him.

18. Bonhoeffer, *Works*, vol. 10, *Barcelona, Berlin, New York 1928–1931*, 459.
19. Bonhoeffer, *Letters and Papers*, 336.
20. Bonhoeffer, *Letters and Papers*, 337.

A Spirituality of Hope

On the one hand, he speaks of the power of the "living Christ" dwelling in the follower of Christ through the sustenance of "the living Holy Spirit."[21] On the other hand, he says that "[Christ] bids us come and die."[22] For Bonhoeffer, receiving and relinquishing are part of the daily contours of the Christian life.

Though those who follow Christ are held in God's beneficent care, they are also buffeted by the realities of life. Living wholly in Christ and wholly in the world, the Christian stands where two "forces" collide—the grace of the kingdom of God and the worldliness of the world. Thus the Christian does not live a charmed life, but a cruciform life that conforms to the way Christ. This life, though marked by grace, is also agonistic, for it groans and longs for the fullness of God's life to come amongst us and to penetrate all aspects of life.

Christian hope, therefore, is not a quiet domain, but is buffeted by great struggles. Though we hope for much in the purposes of God, we may see very little. Bonhoeffer did not see a quick end to Hitler's madness, nor did he see the Confessing Church shine as a light on a hill, nor did he ever get to see or enjoy a life together with his fiancée, Maria.

In referring to the exodus story, Bonhoeffer writes that Moses hoped to enter the promised land, but he died "with great hopes unfulfilled."[23] In speaking of the church, Bonhoeffer points out that hope is the church's "most sacred treasure."[24] Yet the hope of the church does not rest in what it can accomplish on its own, but rather its "object of hope" is in what God can do according to the power and purposes of God.[25]

Despite all the chaos of his day, Bonhoeffer hoped for a post-war world. He explains that in the hope of what God might yet do, it is "possible to reconstruct the life of the nations, both spiritually and materially, on Christian principles."[26]

How we need such hope today!

*We affirm that the biblical gospel is God's
enduring message to our world,
and we determine to defend, proclaim, and embody it. . . .*

---

21. Bonhoeffer, *Cost of Discipleship*, 73.
22. Bonhoeffer, *Cost of Discipleship*, 79.
23. Bonhoeffer, *Works*, vol. 10, *Barcelona, Berlin, New York 1928–1931*, 586.
24. Bonhoeffer, *Works*, vol. 1, *Sanctorum Communio*, 289.
25. Bonhoeffer, *Works*, vol. 1, 154.
26. Bonhoeffer, *Letters and Papers*, 146.

*We affirm that the proclamation of God's kingdom of justice and peace
demands the denunciation of all injustice and oppression,
both personal and structural,
we will not shrink from this prophetic witness.*[27]

---

27. Stott, ed., "Manila Manifesto," in *Making Christ Known*, 231.

10:4

Broken Dreams

Then he said to me, "Mortal, these bones are the whole house of Israel." They say, "Our bones are dried up, and our hope is lost; we are cut off completely."

—Ezekiel 37:11

One of the great challenges in living the Christian life is to discern the will of God in our particular circumstances. We have the wisdom of the biblical narratives, our own expectations, and the faith and hope that God will continue to act in particular ways. But these perspectives don't always coalesce.

We can speak generally about what Scripture reveals about God's wisdom, ways, and how we should live. But we can so easily miss the boat, especially when we add in our own expectations about how we think God should intervene in particular situations.

In looking at Bonhoeffer's life, it is clear that he had a wonderful family. He had musical ability, enjoyed his theological studies, and at a young age, his academic career looked very bright. But after Hitler came to power and with the onset of World War II, Bonhoeffer's life became one of ongoing struggle and broken dreams. Years of his opposition to Hitler eventually led him to years in prison—and finally to his execution.

Yet throughout these life struggles, Bonhoeffer's faith and theological understanding deepened. His adversity did not put him on the road of blaming God, but drew him onto the path of following the suffering Christ into the world. He insists that every Christian "must drink the earthly cup to the dregs."[28] At the same time, he admits his struggle "to banish illusions and fancies from my head."[29]

In Bonhoeffer's prison poems, he acknowledges the blandness of life, describing how "one day turns into another," and each day has "nothing

---

28. Bonhoeffer, *Letters and Papers*, 337.
29. Bonhoeffer, *Letters and Papers*, 215.

new, nothing better."[30] He speaks of feeling "restless and longing and sick, like a bird in a cage."[31] And though he describes himself as "trembling with anger at despotism," he also admits to feeling as a "woebegone weakling."[32]

Amidst this honesty and vulnerability, Bonhoeffer's faith shines. He vows, "thou knowest, O God, I am thine."[33] And he professes, "Christians stand by God in his hour of grieving."[34]

Throughout these dark times, Bonhoeffer trusted God to give him "strength . . . to resist in all the time of distress."[35] He also believed that God would "bring good out of evil" and that we could rely on God to "allay all our fears for the future."[36]

In our present-day world, the life of faith in the West is often one of convenience, lacking in resilience. We tend to proclaim a gospel of blessing rather than a life of discipleship.

Yet in societies marked by poverty and oppression, such as the Majority World of Asia, Africa, and Latin America, Christians understand what it means to follow the way of the suffering Christ. It may now be necessary for them to re-evangelize their fellow Christians in the West!

When we suffer the heartache of broken dreams, it does not mean that God has broken promises, nor does it mean that God no longer cares for us. For in Christ's death, God has already embraced our brokenness; and in Christ's resurrection, God has already given us new life. As Bonhoeffer observes, "the Christian hope of resurrection . . . sends a man [woman] back to his [her] life on earth in a wholly new way."[37]

> *Jesus, by your dying, we are born to new life,*
> *by your anguish and labour we come forth in joy.*
> *Despair turns to hope through your sweet goodness,*
> *through your gentleness, we find comfort in fear. . . .*
> *Lord Jesus, in your mercy heal us,*
> *in your love and tenderness, remake us.*[38]

---

30. Bonhoeffer, *Letters and Papers*, 351.
31. Bonhoeffer, *Letters and Papers*, 348.
32. Bonhoeffer, *Letters and Papers*, 348.
33. Bonhoeffer, *Letters and Papers*, 348.
34. Bonhoeffer, *Letters and Papers*, 349.
35. Bonhoeffer, *Letters and Papers*, 11.
36. Bonhoeffer, *Letters and Papers*, 11.
37. Bonhoeffer, *Letters and Papers*, 336–337.
38. From St. Anselm (c. 1033–1109). Quoted in Ringma and Alexander, eds., *Of*

10:5

Always on the Way

Then he said to them all, "If any want to become my followers, let them deny themselves and take up their cross daily and follow me."
—LUKE 9:23

The Christian life of faith and hope is not about following some ideal, but rather following the way of Christ in the midst of the circumstances of our daily life and the pressing issues of our time. As we follow this way of Christ, we will inevitably find ourselves turning into unexpected side alleys, treading uphill and sliding down, taking circuitous detours, and running into some dead ends. In other words, there is no straight, unwavering line in living the Christian life, for there is always the need to repent, refocus, learn, grow, and change.

Some early Christians described the Christian life as a steady climb up a ladder towards perfection. And some present-day Christians perceive the Christian life as progressing through various stages.

Yet we need to understand our Christian life as a constant process of *putting away* our old ways of being, thinking, and acting so that we can *put on* our new life in Christ. This path of ongoing growth in maturity calls us to embrace a life of ongoing humility and downward mobility. Moreover, this journey of faith and hope must be animated and sustained by the Spirit, for even though we are rooted in Christ, we remain pilgrims *on the way*.

This ongoing journey highlights the fundamental dialectic of the Christian life. We are at "home" in Christ, and we are also at "home" in the world. We are new creations, yet we are still awaiting our full redemption. We are both sinners and saints, both repentant and obedient. We experience joy as well as suffering, momentum and confidence along with fragility and vulnerability.

Martyrs, Monks, and Mystics, 12.

Bonhoeffer knew this precarious journey well. He was certain of the good news in Christ, and he also experienced the cost of discipleship. In his writing, he insists that the gospel must come home to a person "in the spirit of revelation."[39] But he also acknowledges that we need to "risk placing our lives on Jesus' word."[40] He speaks of the lordship of the Spirit, who "would command loyal service to the gospel."[41] And he also points out that the indwelling Spirit can guide the follower of Christ to "do, what he [she] wants to do."[42]

Throughout his writings, Bonhoeffer describes the faith community as a second "incarnation" of Christ, for it is the body of Christ who sings "the song that calls the sinner to turn around, the homeless to come home, the stubborn to weep, and those who weep to rejoice."[43] At the same time, Bonhoeffer worked, prayed, and suffered so that "an authentic worldly order under God's command" could once again flourish.[44]

Bonhoeffer's own life reveals the cruciform pattern of the Christian life, where we are at home in Christ and yet always on the way. All who embark on this journey can experience more growth in the way of Christ, become more prayerful, be more fully led by the Spirit, and seek to more fully love both neighbors and strangers, enemies, and friends.

> *The church is at the very centre*
> *of God's cosmic purpose*
> *and is his appointed means of spreading the Gospel.*
> *But a church which preaches the Cross*
> *must itself be marked by the Cross.*[45]

---

39. Bonhoeffer, *Works*, vol. 9, *Young Bonhoeffer, 1918–1927*, 289.
40. Bonhoeffer, *Works*, vol. 9, 560.
41. Bonhoeffer, *Works*, vol. 9, 268.
42. Bonhoeffer, *Works*, vol. 10, *Barcelona, Berlin, New York 1928–1931*, 448.
43. Bonhoeffer, *Works*, vol. 13, *London 1933–1935*, 357.
44. Bonhoeffer, *Works*, vol. 16, *Conspiracy and Imprisonment 1940–1945*, 532.
45. Stott, ed., "Lausanne Covenant," in *Making Christ Known*, 28.

10:6

God's Final Future

"He will dwell with them;
they will be his peoples,
and God himself will be with them;
he will wipe every tear from their eyes.
Death will be no more;
mourning and crying and pain will be no more,
for the first things have passed away."

—REVELATION 21:3-4

Much of Bonhoeffer's focus was on the here and the now, given the upheaval of his country and the world at large. Indeed, he watched the dark clouds of the threat of war burst into one of the biggest and deadliest conflicts in history. All this gave him much to think and pray about, and he had much to do in the work of resistance as well as his efforts to lay the foundations for a future beyond the chaos of his times.

One might think that Bonhoeffer was so busy that he had no time for study, writing, or prayer. Yet he did all these things, even while acknowledging, "there is simply so much to do."[46]

He speaks of the need for "fervent prayer" and prays that "God will give his witness anew into our hearts."[47] He stresses that a life of "service" is to be expressed "in discipleship."[48] Yet he also insists that the Christian life is marked by joy, for "we learn to delight in Jesus like children."[49]

---

46. Bonhoeffer, *Works*, vol. 15, *Theological Education Underground 1937-1940*, 72.
47. Bonhoeffer, *Works*, vol. 15, 35.
48. Bonhoeffer, *Works*, vol. 15, 218.
49. Bonhoeffer, *Works*, vol. 15, 145.

While Bonhoeffer was deeply involved in the challenges of his time, he always kept the future in view. He believed that he was called to act in the present so that God's good purposes for the future might come about, just as "in Jesus Christ the reality of God entered into the reality of the world."[50]

Bonhoeffer makes it clear that Christians can't just live for God's final purposes in history while denying the call to do the work of love and justice in the here and now. While the ultimate is already scripted, and Christ will one day be all in all, he insists that "the penultimate must be preserved."[51] For as he explains, "the hungry ... needs bread, and the homeless ... needs a roof, the dispossessed need justice, ... the lonely need fellowship, the undisciplined need order, and the slave needs freedom."[52]

Because Christ's salvation, through the Spirit, is for the healing and restoration of the whole world, the past events of Christ's death and resurrection are both a present reality as well as the grand finale in the Christification of heaven and earth in God's final purposes for the whole world.

> *God of joy, we need you now!*
> *Receive our burdens, they are many.*
> *Lift our spirits, they are weighed down. . . .*
> *Grant us grace where shame restricts us.*
> *Grant us life where pain takes hold. . . .*
> *God bless us . . . in the name of the Creator,*
> *the Christ, and the Holy Spirit. Amen.*[53]

---

50. Bonhoeffer, *Ethics*, 192.
51. Bonhoeffer, *Ethics*, 133.
52. Bonhoeffer, *Ethics*, 136.
53. Carvalhaes, *Liturgies from Below*, 320.

Afterword

Some Christians believe that they should only listen to Scripture and to their local pastor or priest to gain direction and inspiration for living the Christian life and serving others. This is understandable, since we are living in a world of competing narratives, multiple perspectives, myriad opinions, and a good dose of conspiracy theories.

Yet it is also not surprising that many Christians feel uncertain or skeptical about whom to listen to or believe.

In this book, I am suggesting that we should *listen* to Dietrich Bonhoeffer. This is a complicated challenge for several reasons. For Roman Catholic readers, Bonhoeffer was a Protestant. To some readers, he was not evangelical. For many, he remains a controversial figure, given his involvement with the German Abwehr, which made various attempts on Hitler's life.

I have not attempted to defend everything that Bonhoeffer wrote or did. Rather, my purpose has been to reflect on his life and writings in order to draw inspiration for our own journey of faith in the twenty-first century. While our times are very different from the madness of Hitler's Third Reich, there is much that is disturbing and challenging in our world.

Amidst these concerns, we are also facing multiple crises in the life of the church, particularly in the West. These include a crisis of personal identity and faith, in communal identity and participation in the faith community, as well as vocational crises in the marketplace and the ministry of the church and church-related institutions.

Moreover, the faith community is experiencing a decline in the significance of prayer, and many churches have "dropped the ball" in terms of spiritual formation, biblical knowledge, and ethics. Many who identify themselves as Christians have little understanding that a life of following Christ involves discipleship and service, let alone suffering.

Churches in the Majority World also face challenges despite their numerical growth. Issues of discipleship and formation in the life of the church and the shaping of a more just social order continue to be pressing issues.

I am certainly not suggesting that these troubling realities can be turned around, nor that there are ready-made answers about how to fix them, for we all live in the mysterious space between God's sovereignty and our human calling and responsibility.

But I do hope that this book offers a pathway of hope. As Bonhoeffer teaches us, renewal is the ongoing work of the Spirit, and we are called to see the "finger" of God in both the life of the church and in other human affairs. So in listening to Bonhoeffer in these pages, I hope we find much to encourage us as we seek to live in the way of Christ in our world.

First and foremost, Bonhoeffer points us to Christ, the Living Word, calling us to live *in* Christ *for* the sake of the world. He challenges the church to be a Christocentric community and insists that our purpose is to live as the body of Christ in the world, beckoning all to embrace the salvation that has already been provided for in Christ. At the same time, we are to challenge the worldliness of the world through prophetic witness.

Bonhoeffer also calls us to prayer and challenges us to embrace a costly discipleship in the way of Christ. He calls the members of the faith community to be willing to suffer for the sake of Christ by seeking to love their neighbors and to work for the restoration of peace and justice in our world.

Moreover, Bonhoeffer reminds us that our life and ministry can be marked by faithful witness rather than the debatable indicators of success. His witness in the face of terrible calamity, amidst the distortion of so many domains of civil life, makes him relevant for our contemporary journey of faith, witness, and service.

Too often, amidst the easy believism of our contemporary Christianity, Christ is not the *center* of our lives, but something we simply "tack on." We want to pursue the worldliness of our world along with the promise of heaven.

Bonhoeffer challenges all of this. As we listen to his voice, we are not seeking a path of sterile imitation, but how the Spirit might stir our imaginations to appropriate his insights into our present-day context.

If we can do this, we will surely be blessed! And having been inspired and nourished by his witness, may we seek to live as a blessing to those around us.

Bibliography

Best, Isabel, ed. *The Collected Sermons of Dietrich Bonhoeffer.* Minneapolis: Fortress, 2012.
Bethge, Eberhard. *Dietrich Bonhoeffer: A Biography.* Rev. ed. Minneapolis: Fortress, 2000.
Bismarck, Ruth-Alice von, and Ulrich Kabitz, eds. *Love Letters from Cell 92: Dietrich Bonhoeffer and Maria von Wedemeyer.* London: Fount, 1994.
Bonhoeffer, Dietrich. *Christ the Center.* Translated by Edwin H. Robertson. New York: HarperSanFrancisco, 1978.
———. *The Cost of Discipleship: Complete Edition.* Translated by R. H. Fuller. London: SCM, 1959.
———. *Dietrich Bonhoeffer Works.* Vol. 1, *Sanctorum Communio,* edited by Joachim von Soosten. Minneapolis: Fortress, 1998.
———. *Dietrich Bonhoeffer Works.* Vol. 4, *Discipleship,* edited by Geffrey B. Kelly and John D. Godsey. Minneapolis: Fortress, 2003.
———. *Dietrich Bonhoeffer Works.* Vol. 5, *Life Together/Prayer Book of the Bible,* edited by Geffrey B. Kelly. Minneapolis: Fortress, 1996.
———. *Dietrich Bonhoeffer Works.* Vol. 8, *Letters and Papers from Prison,* edited by John W. de Gruchy. Minneapolis: Fortress, 2010.
———. *Dietrich Bonhoeffer Works.* Vol. 9, *The Young Bonhoeffer, 1918–1927,* edited by Paul Duane Matheny et al. Minneapolis: Fortress, 2003.
———. *Dietrich Bonhoeffer Works.* Vol. 10, *Barcelona, Berlin, New York 1928–1931,* edited by Clifford J. Green. Minneapolis: Fortress, 2008.
———. *Dietrich Bonhoeffer Works.* Vol. 12, *Berlin 1932–1933,* edited by Larry L. Rasmussen. Minneapolis: Fortress, 2009.
———. *Dietrich Bonhoeffer Works.* Vol. 13, *London 1933–1935,* edited by Keith Clements. Minneapolis: Fortress, 2007.
———. *Dietrich Bonhoeffer Works.* Vol. 15, *Theological Education Underground 1937–1940,* edited by Victoria J. Barnett. Minneapolis: Fortress, 2012.
———. *Dietrich Bonhoeffer Works.* Vol. 16, *Conspiracy and Imprisonment 1940–1945,* edited by Jorgen Glenthoj, Ulrich Kabitz, and Wolf Krotke. Minneapolis: Fortress, 2006.
———. *Ethics.* Translated by Neville Horton Smith. New York: Touchstone, 1995.
———. *Letters and Papers from Prison: The Enlarged Edition.* Edited by Eberhard Bethge. Translated by Reginald H. Fuller and John Bowden. New York: Touchstone, 1997.
———. *Life Together.* Translated by John W. Doberstein. New York: HarperSanFrancisco, 1954.
Carvalhaes, Claudio. *Liturgies from Below.* Nashville: Abingdon, 2020.

Bibliography

Celebrating Common Prayer: A Version of The Daily Office SSF. London: Mowbray, 1994.
Common Worship: Services and Prayers for the Church of England. London: Church House, 2000.
de Gruchy, John W., ed. *The Cambridge Companion to Dietrich Bonhoeffer.* Cambridge: Cambridge University Press, 1999.
Green, Clifford J. *Bonhoeffer: A Theology of Sociality.* Rev. ed. Grand Rapids: Eerdmans, 1999.
Guder, Darrell, ed. *Missional Church.* Grand Rapids: Eerdmans, 1998.
Haynes, Stephen R. *The Bonhoeffer Phenomenon: Portraits of a Protestant Saint.* Minneapolis: Fortress, 2004.
Joint Document of the Pontifical Council for Interreligious Dialogue and the Congregation for Evangelization of Peoples. "Dialogue and Proclamation: Reflection and Orientations on Interreligious Dialogue and the Proclamation of the Gospel of Jesus Christ." Posted on Vatican website, May 19, 1991.
Kelly, Geffrey B., and F. Burton Nelson. *The Cost of Moral Leadership: The Spirituality of Dietrich Bonhoeffer.* Grand Rapids: Eerdmans, 2003.
McLaren, Brian. *A Generous Orthodoxy.* Grand Rapids: Zondervan, 2006.
Moltmann, Jürgen. *The Church in the Power of the Spirit.* Philadelphia: Fortress, 1993.
Morley, Janet, ed. *Bread of Tomorrow: Prayers for the Church Year.* Maryknoll, NY: Orbis, 1992.
The Northumbria Community. *Celtic Daily Prayer: Book Two.* New York: HarperOne, 2002.
Rahner, Karl. *The Shape of the Church to Come.* New York: Seabury, 1974.
Rilke, Rainer Maria. *Letters to a Young Poet.* Rev. ed. Translated by M.D. Herter Norton. New York: Norton, 1993.
Ringma, Charles R. "Bonhoeffer's Passion for Renewing the Church and its Witness in Troubled Times." In *In the Midst of Much-Doing: Cultivating a Missional Spirituality,* 277–304. Carlisle, UK: Langham Global Library, 2023.
———. "A Critical Evaluation of the Ecclesiology of Dietrich Bonhoeffer." BD thesis, Reformed Theological College, Geelong, Australia, 1986.
———. "Dietrich Bonhoeffer: His Life, Theology, Praxis with Implications for Ecumenism." *Phronesis* 4.1 (1997) 21–32.
———. "In the World and Sore Afraid: Dietrich Bonhoeffer and Living in Fearful Times." In *Fear and Faith: Christian, Jewish and Evolutionary Perspectives,* edited by Rachael Kohn, 1–12. Adelaide, SA: ATF, 2019.
———. *Seize the Day with Dietrich Bonhoeffer.* Sutherland, NSW: Albatross, 1991; Colorado Springs: NavPress/Pinon, 2000.
Ringma, Charles, and Irene Alexander, eds. *Of Martyrs, Monks, and Mystics: A Yearly Meditational Reader of Ancient Spiritual Wisdom.* Eugene, OR: Cascade, 2015.
Scherer, James A., and Stephen B. Bevans, eds. *New Directions in Mission and Evangelization 1: Basic Statements 1974–1991.* Maryknoll, NY: Orbis, 1992.
Smith, C. Christopher, and John Pattison. *Slow Church.* Downers Grove, IL: InterVarsity, 2014.
Stevens, R. Paul. *Liberating the Laity.* Vancouver: Regent College Publishing, 1985.
Stott, John, ed. *Making Christ Known: Historic Mission Documents from the Lausanne Movement, 1974–1989.* Grand Rapids: Eerdmans, 1996.

www.ingramcontent.com/pod-product-compliance
Lightning Source LLC
Chambersburg PA
CBHW031429150426
43191CB00006B/459